Wooden Valley

A Teacher's Memoir

Donna Reid Connell

Wooden Valley

Our whole family drove out to check the site for
my new job at Wooden Valley.

Wooden Valley

A Teacher's Memoir

Donna Reid Connell Ed.D.

Writers Club Press
San Jose New York Lincoln Shanghai

Wooden Valley
A Teacher's Memoir

Writers Club Press
an imprint of iUniverse.com, Inc.

For information address:
iUniverse.com, Inc.
5220 S 16th, Ste. 200
Lincoln, NE 68512
www.iuniverse.com

ISBN: 0-595-19397-8

Printed in the United States of America

Dedication

As a former journalist I have always written about the here and now. My former neighbor, Jessamyn West, the author of *Friendly Persuasion,* which was made into a movie, and other books about her Quaker background, repeated to me several times that I should write about events of the past as she had successfully done. Her jovial husband, retired school superintendent Dr. Harry McPherson, agreed. *Then no one will still be alive to check your facts!*

The events in Wooden Valley occurred over forty years ago. This is how I remember that experience. Names of most of the students have been changed to protect their privacy. If they read this they will recognize themselves.

Education is not the filling
of a pail,
But the lighting of a fire.
William Butler Yeats

Contents

Foreword

For those who long for "the good old days," when teaching was simpler, Donna Connell's delightful reminiscence, *Wooden Valley: A Teacher's Memoir,* will shatter that illusion entertainingly. We've all known challenging students, but few as direct as first-grader Johnny who said, "I'm not going to learn to read and you can't make me." How and why Donna was able to succeed with Johnny is a fun detective yarn.

Donna writes about what she knows best–teaching "in the trenches." Donna's early teaching credentials were limited to her experience with her own preschool-age children–a far cry from the special education students, ages 6–22, that showed up for her first class, housed in a barn. From such humble beginnings with so little preparation, you'll follow Donna's journey to becoming one of California's most respected early language-acquisition consultants.

How to teach young children to read has been a topic of heated debate for the last 40 years. Should we rely primarily on phonics, sight words, or language experience? Many well-respected researchers have weighed in on this issue, which seems to have come full circle back to phonics at the present time. Nonetheless, despite the research, we don't have all the answers, because legions of young children continue to struggle with the printed word. Remediation programs, from Reading Recovery to peer tutoring, abound in schools, and private reading clinics and tutors outside of school have become a cottage industry.

Donna's work with young children led her to develop a method that works, no matter what theory of reading is currently in vogue. Her story is the story of how she taught hundreds of children to read, moving them naturally along the continuum from Scribble to Scrabble. This journey, with all of its travails and triumphs along the way, is the saga of the last 40 years of education. Anyone who has ever taught will relate to and love this book.

Barbara Nemko, Ph.D.
Napa County Superintendent of Schools

Acknowledgments

I am indebted to Lilburn Clark and the rest of the Wooden Valley School Board who hired me to teach their children in spite of the fact that I had no teaching credential and no experience in the field. There were no administrators or other teachers at this one room rural school to offer any advice. I was totally on my own. Without this school board's faith in me I would not have had that one wonderful year where I learned to be a teacher totally through trial and error and on the job learning.

Could ignorance be a personal strength in times of crisis? Poets in former centuries have suggested that ignorance has value.

In the last century Bayard Taylor encouraged his daughter:
> *Learn to live, and live to learn,*
> *Ignorance like a fire doth burn.*
> *Little tasks make large return.*

In the century before him Thomas Gray discouraged clear thinking:
> *Thought would destroy their paradise.*
> *No more; where ignorance is bliss,*
> *'Tis folly to be wise.*

Before Wooden Valley

I'M NOT GOING TO LEARN TO READ,
AND YOU CAN'T MAKE ME DO IT!

This vehement outburst was my introduction to pint-sized Johnny as he arrived for his first day at Wooden Valley School. It was my first day too as teacher of this one-room rural school in a small farming community separated from the larger Napa Valley by a mountain named George. Having lived on the side of George for five years I was familiar with its terrain and on a first name relationship with it. No one seemed to know if George ever had a last name.

Until Johnny's arrival my greeting ritual was to stand on the porch at the front of the school, shake the hand of each student as they arrived, introduce myself as the new teacher, and dismiss the children to the adjoining playground until official morning opening time.

Johnny had been delivered to school in a noisy black truck, obviously way too big for the narrow, two-lane country road in front of the school. I watched as this youngster pushed two smaller boys, probably his siblings, to the floor of the open truck bed. Then he smoothly vaulted over the side rail and landed in the thick dust beside the road. Stomping the dust from his new boots he marched up to me and refused my outstretched hand. *Are you the new teacher?* My head bobbed up and down as I introduced myself. He planted himself spread-legged in front of me. *I'm Johnny. I'm in first grade.*

I'M NOT GOING TO LEARN TO READ,
AND YOU CAN'T MAKE ME DO IT !

1

Some fleeting thoughts and a bit of panic jumped around in my brain. How did I get into this teaching business? I looked over to the playground where seventeen other children with an age spread of six to twelve were impatiently waiting for me to shake the ancient brass bell to announce the beginning of this first day of the school year. Did they suspect that I had no teaching credential, no experience in the field and had taken no college courses in what they called Education? Do veteran teachers know how to deal with Johnnys?

How did I wind up as a teacher in my middle years? Certainly this was not part of my life goal. Nearing my third birthday I planned to be a carrot. My older sister, Catherine, attended kindergarten where she was exposed to what they called, children's diseases. First she shared chicken pox with me. Next she brought home whooping cough. Measles was my undoing. The fever went higher and higher until finally the rash broke through.

Shortly after, our parents were moving to a new house one weekend and sent Catherine and me to our grandparents so we would not be in the way. The first evening I was sitting on Grandpa's lap and began to shiver. Then Nanny wrapped me in a blanket and sat with me in front of their pot-bellied stove. When the chill continued she phoned old Dr. Doran who had delivered me almost three years before. Soon we heard him chugging up in his new Model T Ford. His horse and buggy had been retired. My diagnosis was pneumonia, probably induced by being so run-down from chicken pox, whooping cough and measles in a row before I recovered from each one. No one suggested that I be hospitalized because that's where people were sent to die. Instead Grandpa's big oak Morris chair was flattened to improvise a crib for me. They placed it next to an open window for maximum fresh air to help me breathe. My fever stayed at 106 degrees for a week. I heard Dr. Doran telling Nanny that so many brain cells must be burned out that if I lived through the high fever I would probably be a vegetable. That was when I decided to be a carrot.

Each day I checked my skin to see if it was turning orange. I did recover and stayed being a little girl and did not turn into a carrot.

After attending the circus my next life plan was to be an acrobat and float through the air on the flying trapeze. My constantly blistered and calloused hands from frequent practice on the rings and bars at school were evidence of my drive. At that time girls only wore dresses. So because I was upside down so much of the time Mom always bought an extra yard or two of fabric when she made a dress for me. The extra fabric was for matching pants, which did not look like underpants.

BECOMING A WRITER

Then in junior high I won a prize in a citywide contest for a book report. I would be a writer! I would travel to far away places and write about my dangerous adventures.

THAT'S ABSURD! THIS COUNTRY IS NOT AT WAR! My exasperated mother was ridiculing my announcement that my eventual career goal was to be a war correspondent. WE WILL BE WHEN I GRADUATE FROM COLLEGE was my angry retort. COLLEGE! Our family, like the rest of the nation was still feeling the effects of the Depression years. I was expected to go to the public business school and become a secretary in order to get a safe civil service job as my sister had done.

Dad finally agreed that we could afford the twenty-six dollars tuition for each semester at the University of California. I could live at home and, because the bus fee was ten cents each way, I could walk the three miles to the campus. Somehow I did need to earn sixty dollars each semester to pay for the required books for whatever courses I would take.

If I were to be a war correspondent, I had to start getting some newspaper experience, so I found a job in the Berkeley circulation office of the San Francisco Chronicle. One of my tasks was to soothe the irate parents of the carriers. They believed that the office manager was cheating their children out of their earnings. He was a Fagan type, right out of a Dickens novel. His name was Pop Korn.

In addition to my office job, Pop helped me initiate a shopping news for Saturday morning delivery in North Berkeley. He showed me how to use some ancient printing equipment in the back of the office. I hired the mother of a friend to sell my advertising space in order to present a more mature and responsible appearing front sales person. Then I hired six neighbor boys for distribution. My masthead in big black type shouted, GOOD MORNING.

My shopping news was a successful venture for about six months. After I paid Pop Korn for paper and printing ink, my advertising sales person and my six carrier boys there was still sufficient funds left over to purchase books for two semesters at the University. Apparently I was too successful. One Saturday morning a counterfeit shopping news blaring, GOOD MORNING, on its masthead appeared at front doors throughout the area. A large local market had taken advantage of a novice and usurped my successful product. That was the end of that publishing venture.

Another requirement for my war correspondent career was to take journalism courses. But for economy in the Depression years the University had eliminated this department. In its place the campus newspaper, the Daily Californian, had a four-year apprentice system. Without a journalism faculty, the freshman reporters were trained by the sophomores, they by the juniors, and finally up to the half dozen senior editors who survived the system.

For three years, until we reached that senior goal, we were expected to appear at the Daily Californian office every afternoon at 3:00 for writing assignments from our superiors. The selected junior and senior staff stayed on the job until the paper was put to bed on the presses around 1:00 a.m. Somehow we managed to have enough energy left over to take enough courses and fulfill requirements to graduate.

The summer before my senior year I was actually hired to work on a real newspaper in Vallejo, 30 miles north of my home in Berkeley. My aunt who lived there agreed to provide bed and board. I was to replace the person in charge of the women's page who was on a three months vacation.

My first assignment was to sell advertising space celebrating June high school graduation. The management expected me to sell to merchants, such as jewelers and stationers, who would then profit from this event. In my naiveté and unfamiliarity with this navy town adjoining Mare Island Naval Base, I sold all the space to the bars on the waterfront, mostly those with girls available upstairs. The editor was in a bit of hot water with the natives when my *Congratulations to the Graduates* sheet was printed. But he kept me on anyway for the rest of the summer.

During my years on the Daily Californian the top post of editor was not available to women students. That discriminatory practice didn't change until World War II when there was a shortage of eligible men for the position. At that time most of the young men took time out from college to get in either Army, Navy, Marine, or Coast Guard uniform in order to save the world for Democracy. Clawing my way to the top spot available on the Cal, I finally was appointed Women's Editor for the '36-'37 year with a column on the editorial page to fill five days a week. This assignment came with a small salary, so I quit my job with Pop Korn. My column's logo was a wolf and girl cartoon with the title, *Little Reid Writing Good.* At the end of the year the Blue and Gold college annual reported that my column took no neutral stands. Instead it shouted either *Rah Rah How Wonderful,* or *Down With Everything.*

Mom was right. Graduation came and our country was still not at war, so my war correspondent career was shelved. I was a runner-up in a year long fashion writing contest by Vogue magazine. First prize was a year on their staff in Paris. Second prize was a year on their staff in New York. I came in third, which meant honorable mention and my picture in Vogue.

Four young men who had just graduated from Yale saw my name and my picture and hired me as their Girl Friday. They had been college journalists and were bravely attempting to establish a New Yorker type magazine for the West, with San Francisco as their headquarters. They named it *COAST.*

Our office was on the top floor of a six-story 15-foot wide building squeezed between two skyscrapers. When the editors needed to talk privately in this cramped space they used a secret language they had invented in college. The building's elevator operator was convinced they must be planning some dire subservient activity and kept insisting that I should leave. Hearing the strange language daily, I gradually began to understand some of the words. Whenever I turned in a manuscript to any of the editors he said, *nimblesbee,* which I assumed to mean, *thank you.* I filled two pages each month with items aimed at women readers, acted as secretary, receptionist and door keeper, and previewed all manuscripts submitted to the magazine before passing some on to the editors.

To encourage advertisers, one of my tasks was to survey San Francisco stores in order to recommend some new items available. After my monthly shopping column had appeared several times with my byline, *Donna Reid,* a new actress appeared on the Hollywood scene with my name but slightly different spelling, *Donna Reed.* Years later she was the guest on Ralph Edwards' *This is Your Life* television program. When she was asked if this was her given name or her stage name she explained that her agent copied it from a byline in a San Francisco magazine, no doubt mine. Her real name was *Donnabelle Mullinger,* not particularly catchy.

A dark, muscular young man with an Armenian sounding name came to our office regularly, sat on the edge of my desk and cockily told me each time he came that soon he would be recognized as a famous writer. Meantime, he probably could not afford a bath or a haircut. His odor was so offensive that I was certain his manuscripts must be trash. The editors never saw them because I automatically returned them with rejection slips. He was right. The following year I found his name, William Saroyan, on a best selling book jacket. Years later I saw a life-size brass bust of Saroyan in front of an elaborate conference center dedicated to him. He looked just the same, with a thick beard and long, shaggy hair. I could almost smell him.

I needed more excitement in my slowly budding writing career. Maybe I would find it in the advertising business. One of the stores I mentioned in my shopping column was a prestigious homewares store. They hired me to write advertising copy about their china, crystal and silver. The manager of the kitchen department asked me to feature a dangerous looking tool in a three by four inch space on our next full-page ad. He had barrels of them in the basement and wanted to make room for new items. In my ad I described this tomahawk-like tool with a cast metal head with two ends. The hatchet end had three sharp points like a crown. The opposite end had a dozen short dull points on a solid square bed. My copy described its innumerable, versatile uses, including chops ice, breaks bones, cracks nuts and tenderizes meat. No home should be without one. *And all for twenty-five cents!* I did not mention its obvious possibilities as a weapon. The next morning there was a block-long line of customers waiting for the store to open. We sold out my tool in the first half-hour. It was a heady success. My words had power!

A small group of journalists, recent graduates of the University, met regularly on Friday evenings for relaxation and fellowship. At one of these get-togethers we decided to pool our skills and develop a new product. A following discussion revealed the few available choices at that time in breakfast cereals—only Corn Flakes, Shredded Wheat, Puffed Rice, Puffed Wheat and something called, Muffets. Our nation was obviously in desperate need of a new cereal.

One couple's subsequent research on grains at the library indicated the nutritional value of oats, so we decided to feature that one. On the packaging committee, I helped design a yellow box with blue lettering and wrote the copy for it. Finishing our recipe, we met to cook up the trial samples of our product. Putting my tongue in the hole of a LIFESAVER in my mouth, I suggested putting a hole in those first dabs of goop ready for the oven. Finding a skewer, our cook poked a hole in each oat drop. A beer cap snapped open, followed by a toast, CHEERS! Someone mumbled, *cheery oats.* Then noticing the round shape of our product, he burst out with a name for it, CHEERY O'S.

Two weeks later we presented our original product as guests of the prestigious San Francisco Advertising Club who gave us a standing ovation. Praise was our only reward. We had mixed feelings when six months later our cereal appeared on the market, changing the spelling of our name to *Cheerios.* In recent years when the manufacturer celebrated *Cheerios* fiftieth birthday they erroneously mentioned in the press that it had been developed originally by some *unknown college students.*

My war correspondent career goal seemed a little doubtful. Germany, Italy and Japan were cruelly invading others' territories, but our country was remaining neutral. Instead, a traveling salesman named John convinced me to marry him and move to the southwest where I could write about the desert. When President Roosevelt did declare war on Japan my personal obligations were to my new husband and our newborn first child. It was too late for me. In the evening news I saw a photo of Marguerite Higgins, two years behind me at the Daily Californian and in whom I had invested hours of training to become a journalist. She had become a war correspondent instead of me and was riding in a jeep with an army general whom she later married.

THE WAR YEARS

We were eating lunch in our new house in Phoenix when President Roosevelt announced over the radio that the Japanese had attacked Pearl Harbor. All patriotic Americans were expected to assist, so John decided to join the Navy. Within two weeks we sold our house, shipped most of our possessions to our parents in California, and boarded a train for the East Coast where John was ordered for training.

Most of our baggage for the cross-country trip was necessary equipment for our month old first born son, James Richard. We started calling him J.R., which eventually slurred into Jerry. John's first orders required that he report in *blues* with one gold stripe on each sleeve for the Ensign rank. Arizona, being inland, had no facilities for purchasing navy uniforms. We were scheduled for a three-hour lay over when we changed trains in Chicago and assumed this would be enough time to buy the required uniforms.

Our train arrived late in Chicago, cutting the planned shopping time in half. A taxi whisked us to Marshall Fields, the only store whose name was familiar to us. When John explained our urgent needs to the nearest salesman in the men's department someone pushed the fast forward button. Two blue uniforms and two khaki uniforms in the right size magically appeared. Tailors rushed out, pinned the sleeves and the pants cuffs, and then disappeared into their sewing stations for the necessary alterations. We filled the short waiting time shopping for the required cap, cap covers in white and khaki, black ties and socks, gold bars for the shirts, shoulder bars with one gold stripe and the brass buttons for the coats. Still on fast forward, a tailor led us down a freight elevator then ran out in the middle of Chicago traffic to hail a cab for us. Our taxi driver found the eastbound train with the right number and helped us carry on our boxed uniforms, the baby and the baby equipment just as the conductor called out, *ALL ABOARD!*

Later in the afternoon, as our train headed east, John opened some of his boxes to try to put the many parts of his uniforms together. In our rush at Marshall Fields they had forgotten to include the brass buttons. John tried on his coat and cap, then put on a one man comedy routine, pretending to report for duty while saluting with one hand and holding his double breasted coat together with the other. While waiting in the station in Springfield, Massachusetts, for our transfer to a local train to take us to our destination in New Hampshire, John shared his button problem with a young marine. He obligingly took off his cap to show the name of a uniform store in Boston, which might supply our needs.

For the last leg of our journey we boarded the local train and found that it had no hot water. There was no way to warm Jerry's bottle. When we stopped at each small town along the way John raced to the nearest coffee shop, asked someone to plunge the bottle into warm water, then ran back to the train holding the bottle in his armpit to retain any heat. After three of these pit stops the formula was no longer icy. By this time Jerry was so upset and shrieking with hunger that he gulped the contents. He then created an amazing milk explosion shooting his formula over us and any other travelers within six feet of us. This messy scene was replayed over and over again until we reached Hanover, where John was to be magically turned into a navy officer at Dartmouth College.

John was assigned to a room in a student dormitory. There was no designated housing for wives because women were supposed to stay at home. Renting the top floor of a hundred-year old house across the river in Vermont, we closed the doors on eight of the ten rooms so the ghosts wouldn't wander about at night. That left a huge kitchen and one bedroom for Jerry and me.

I wrote to the military uniform company in Boston to order some Ensign's buttons for John's uniforms. In three weeks their answer came back, *Ensign's buttons are the same as Admiral's buttons, so we didn't send any.* Fortunately one of John's roommates had a second set so John didn't have to report for duty doing his two-handed comedy routine.

In six weeks John learned how to send and receive messages with signal flags, climb ropes, tie knots, salute properly, steer and dock a ship, find his way around an ocean, shoot pistols and rifles, and mostly how to march. He was instructed to reveal only his name, rank and serial number if captured. Because his occupation before the war was a western states representative for a major fountain pen company, the Navy assigned him to be a communication officer. He would send and receive messages in military codes. Whoever had determined this assignment did not seem to know or care that John's background was in sales, not communications, and that his own code for spelling was inventive. We hoped he would not be responsible for sinking one of our ships by signaling *zig* instead of *zag*.

John's first assignment was to the Pentagon for further training. Washington was so overcrowded with military personnel that housing was at a premium. John's stepfather's nephew, whose family lived in a thirteen-foot row house in Virginia, generously took us in. The upstairs thirteen feet was divided into two bedrooms. We three occupied one of them. The second one held our benefactor's two children and the family's live-in maid. It was obvious we were in the way, so John booked a night flight for Jerry and me back to my parent's home in California. The plane was fully occupied and there was no place to lay Jerry down. I fell asleep holding him. When the light from the morning sun awakened me somewhere over Arizona, he was gone. The flight attendant told me that she rescued Jerry from a fall to the cabin floor and gave him to the pilot to hold. Not yet three months old, Jerry already had two thousand miles of flight time as co-pilot.

Eventually, after learning the necessary codes for his assignment, John was assigned to an office in San Francisco where he was to send and receive messages from ships in the Pacific. We retrieved our belongings from our parents and bought a small house in Berkeley. John wanted me to have that security in case he did not return from his pending overseas assignment. The months dragged on, then a year, always waiting. One of our closest friends was listed as killed during the infamous Bataan march in the Philippines. Then two of my college friends became widows when their young husbands went to the ocean's bottom in submarines.

Our daughter, Lucinda Anne, soon known as Cindy, was born during this waiting time. In contrast to our easy going Jerry, who had just celebrated his second birthday, Cindy required constant supervision. From her first days she asserted her independence. She kicked off her blankets. Then, as she matured, she climbed out of her clothes, her crib, her high-chair, then windows, disappearing in the night, an accomplished escape artist. While John was on duty one night I was awakened at 4:00 in the morning by loud banging and yelling coming from outside. Racing to the bedroom window I saw our two-year old Cindy hanging upside down from our picket fence. Apparently she had awakened, slipped out her window, dropped to the patio and climbed the fence. She was suspended by one foot caught between the pickets and loudly protesting her predicament. After that incident we nailed her window shut.

An official phone call from the Navy one January evening told me that the dreaded time had come. John would ship out some time during the week. His destination was necessarily a military secret. Because of security we could not even say goodbye. To pass the next lonely months, a friend from our former home in Arizona invited me to spend the summer at their children's horse camp in the mountains. The desert was too hot for their horses, so they closed their Phoenix riding school for the summer and moved the horses to a cooler climate. My family warned that it would be dangerous for me to drive alone across both the California and Arizona deserts with my two small youngsters. But I had a reliable car, which John had purchased for his traveling job before the war began. Also I demonstrated to them my efficiency and independence by learning to change a tire in case of a flat.

It was a long but uneventful three-day trip. The children and I arrived safely at the camp set in a pine forest in northern Arizona. There was a horse for every camper. The children's last names read like a Who's Who in America. The night we arrived the camp was in an uproar because Ian, the youngest one of three Rockefeller children, was lost. Fortunately he stayed on a road and they found him in the morning.

My two children and I slept in a tent away from the regular bunkhouse. In the middle of one night a heavy electrical storm washed away the tent pegs. The canvas tent roof settled down until it rested on the sidebars of Cindy's crib. In the morning, when the sun warmed the earth around us there was the most amazing sight. Toadstools as big as dinner plates kept popping up around us, no doubt encouraged by the loose pine duff which had been enriched by horse manure. They were red with large white polka dots, like illustrations in books of nursery rhymes. Jerry called them fairy toadstools and we would not have been surprised to find some little elves using them for furniture.

My assigned job was as the camp's purchasing agent. Several times a week I drove into town for groceries or other needed items such as mail. On one trip a large cougar ran across the road in front of my car. After that I moved our tent closer to the other camp buildings. It was a quiet summer, but I didn't completely escape the trauma of the war. One day I returned from town with an official notice from the war department for the owners of the horse camp. Their son, a pilot, had been shot down, but was uninjured in a German prison camp.

The Japanese surrender came in August and I retraced my route back to Berkeley to await John's return, but he was not relieved until December. When he jumped off the steps of the Santa Fe in Berkeley his crumpled khaki uniform had a chest full of bright ribbons. Miraculously he was whole. The only visible change was evident when his cap fell off in our rush to hold each other. There was a little more space between his curly black hair and his eyebrows. Jerry remembered his dad. But to Cindy, John was a stranger who had come to live with us. It was six months before she accepted him as a member of our family.

Luxury items, such as fountain pens, were limited during the war years because the manufacturers were making items related to the war effort. Then, after the war, there was a big demand for such indulgences. So John reluctantly returned to his traveling job, selling to jewelers and stationers in three western states. Again he became the stranger who visited us every third weekend. Whenever he was home we talked about our need to make a life change so we could really be together as a family. We knew the time for a change had come when our second daughter, Mary Elizabeth, who later named herself, Mimi, was born. John missed it all. He was two hundred miles away, so our next door neighbor took me to the hospital.

THE RANCH YEARS

Even though he came home with his physical body intact, John was still torn inside with the trauma of the maimed, the dead, and the destruction he had witnessed. Perhaps, we thought, a move to the clean, fresh air of some rural place would supply the healing. A move away from city life might give us that opportunity.

Neither of us had ever lived in anything but a house on a twenty-five foot lot in a big city. Moving to the country would be not only an adventure, but also a challenge. My only experience with animals was raising a goldfish from its egg given to me by a neighbor. John's family had let him keep a stray German Shepherd dog. In addition, having majored in zoology at college, he did know something about the anatomy of birds and animals. He quit his traveling job and we started our real adventure.

We bought a seven-acre ranch on the base of the mountain called George, part of the eastern slope of Napa Valley. The steepest part of our acreage was typical of California foothills, forested with valley oaks, buckeyes and digger pines. Closer to the ground was a maze of bushes with shiny, smooth bark and perfectly round bright red berries. The early Spanish explorers named this bush, *manzanita*, little apple.

Our farmhouse had been placed at the bottom of our property where it was not so steep. One and one-half stories, with a screened porch across the front, it gave the impression that it might tip forward at any time onto the road below. Long ago our house had been painted green, but was faded to almost gray, with a dull green cast. Inside there were a large farm kitchen, a smaller central room, two small bedrooms divided by a narrow stairway which led to the attic with a five foot ceiling, and a bathroom with a claw-foot tub. An enormous, ceiling high, noisy oil heater occupied the center of the middle room. Each of our children had its own space. Jerry slept on the screened porch. Cindy's room was the attic. Mimi, the baby, occupied one of the bedrooms and we the other. We put our old upright piano near the back door, the only place where the flooring could support its weight. I painted the piano Dutch blue to match the kitchen.

We moved in on the first of February. It had rained heavily the week before, so there were rivulets of muddy water draining off the mountain. In the middle of our first night Mimi started braying like a donkey—the dreaded croup. Having experienced this scary ailment in Jerry's infancy, I knew she needed steam in a hurry to aid her breathing. Wrapping her in a blanket, I turned on all the hot water faucets in the bathroom. We sat there until she could breathe freely again. In the morning we all dressed in a circle around the oil heater, but the house wouldn't get warm. Investigating the problem, John discovered that the rain's run-off from the mountain had settled in our basement and frozen into a room-sized cake of ice. Jerry and Cindy had their own private skating rink for several days.

It was necessary to decide how to earn a living in this new setting. Our mountainside was too steep for profitably growing most crops. The wine industry had not yet spread through the valley, so we did not consider growing grapes. We were still escaping from wartime killing, so raising animals or poultry for their meat was outvoted. Our solution was to produce eggs with the help of a quantity of cooperative hens. Egg ranchers in the area advised us that, to make a living for our family, we would need a minimum of three thousand hens.

Solitary confinement was the suggested housing for the hens because chickens, like people, apparently develop some social problems in crowded conditions. The recommendations were explicit. Each hen should be housed in an individual wire cage so the hens would not peck at each other. The wire floor of each cage should slant so that eggs would roll forward into a gathering trough. Then, walking along each aisle of cages, we could easily fill our buckets with eggs to sell. It all sounded simple enough for amateurs, so our chicken adventure began.

We bought enormous rolls of wire netting, some lumber and some tools. With this equipment, John cleverly engineered our first condominium for one thousand hens. Stretching across our slope for three hundred and sixty feet and covered with an aluminum roof, it looked like a huge, shiny airplane had landed on our hillside. Later, John would manufacturer two more of these.

To the delight of the children, we bought our first fifty day-old chicks, guaranteed to be all girls. The hatchery employed some Japanese specialists who determined the sex of chicks by some secret way of squeezing them as they emerged from their eggs. The unfortunate boy chicks then would be sold to grow into chicken dinners. Our yellow balls of fluff had to be kept at a temperature near one hundred degrees Fahrenheit. We had no suitable outbuildings for the survival of newly hatched chicks and the floors of our house were too cold. Setting up a card table next to our bed seemed a suitable alternative. John taped a cardboard fence around the edge of the table. Then we kept our bedside lamp burning night and day over the chicks to supply the necessary warmth. We were so tired at night that the light, the damp smell and the constant peeping didn't keep us awake.

When the chicks began to jump from their card table residence onto our bed we knew that a move for them was necessary. By this time they had grown more feathers for warmth. We arranged a spot for them in our pump house until they were old enough to live in their new solitary out-door cages. The hatchery sex experts made two major errors. Even we amateurs knew that two of the chicks were boys when they began to grow bright pink combs on their heads. Knowing these were to be our first home grown dinners, we warned the children not to name the boy chicks so as not to become attached to them.

John joined a group of other egg ranchers who met one evening a week for advice from the agricultural extension service connected to the University. At these classes he learned how to be the executioner. He was able to reconcile the idea of butchering the chicks with the necessity of feeding his family. Following instructions, when the male chicks matured sufficiently for eating, he held each rooster's head in one hand, the body with the other, then pulled them apart until he felt the neck bones snap. I didn't look. We roasted and ate our roosters with just a little bit of guilt.

Though being a farmer's wife was not one of my early life goals, I was learning to play the role. My long days were spent in canning apricots and applesauce from our trees, delivering eggs to market where my kids ran loose hiding from each other in the mountains of feed sacks, hoeing weeds in the garden patch, and inventing new chicken and egg recipes. A chicken and pasta recipe I concocted, which I named, Chicketti, was printed in a San Francisco paper. I only received honorable mention, not a cash prize. In our former life style John had come home to us only every third weekend. Now he took a break from his ranch chores at mid-morning every day and expected me to have hot coffee and a snack ready for him. Adjusting to living together twenty-four hours a day was part of our chosen package of country life.

Of course we had to get a dog. My requirements were that it be big enough to scare off intruders, but gentle enough so it wouldn't frighten me. We chose a loveable Irish Setter pup and registered her officially as Scarlet Patricia of Mount George. Raising dogs might supplement the income from our egg business, so at the proper time we introduced Pat to a charming male Irish Setter who lived in the neighborhood.

Pat slept on the screened porch with Jerry. About 4:00 a.m. after a busy Halloween night, we were awakened by a desperate *MOTHERRRRR!* Answering Jerry's frantic alarm, we rushed to the porch. Pat had found a warm soft spot to deliver her pups. Seven squirming duplicates of Pat were in Jerry's bed. We lifted him out so he wouldn't squash them and let Pat have the bed for the rest of the night. By daylight she had delivered four more pups. We awoke the girls so they could watch the last ones being born and participate in this miracle of birth.

Mother dogs are usually equipped for feeding only eight pups at a time, so our veterinarian advised us that for both Pat's health and the pups' we should dispose of three of her eleven immediately. Which ones? Here we were into killing again. John reluctantly drowned three pups in our laundry tubs. Then, when milk kept running out of the nose of two of the surviving pups we found that they had a cleft palate. They also went into the laundry tubs, leaving Pat with six.

We asked the owner of the pups' father for her dog's official papers so we could register the pups. Her dog had never been registered, so we could not ask top price for our beautiful puppies. Five of them went quickly to good homes. No one wanted the sixth, so we kept him and gave him a proper Irish name. Clancy was huge, more like a Great Dane than a Setter, with an appetite to match. He claimed all cracked eggs he found under the hen cages as his own. When Mimi, now aged two, went wandering outside I could always locate her by Clancy's tail like a red flag in the air. He was always at her heels in case she had a snack to share.

At the foot of our driveway was a small empty reservoir, which a former tenant had filled with rusting metal junk, including vast rolls of barbed wire. Late one afternoon we heard Clancy's cries of distress from the reservoir. Always clumsy, perhaps he had fallen in, or he might have jumped in out of curiosity. At any rate his inability to get out was most disturbing to him. He was bleeding in several places from jumping against the barbed wire and frothing at the mouth. Fearing rabies, we hesitated to rescue him. The nearest veterinarian responded to our emergency and bravely entered the reservoir with a hypodermic needle. Clancy was quickly tranquilized, lifted from his prison and taken to the dog hospital. The next day when we brought him home the diagnosis was a major seizure brought on by severe stress. Our veterinarian warned us that Clancy would probably always show signs of brain damage. He never was very bright anyway, but we loved him just the same.

Neither John nor I had any experience with young children before we had our own, but with three we were beginning to get the hang of it. Before we moved to the ranch both Jerry and Cindy attended a parent-cooperative preschool, which gave us more of an insight into improving our parenting expertise. In our isolated rural setting it became more of a need for Mimi. With ten other families on the eastern slope of the valley, we initiated the formation of a play-group. This loose association gradually developed into a parent-cooperative preschool. We rented the lower floor of the local farm center building and hired a teacher. Then each family served the school in various capacities: maintenance, creating materials, bookkeeping and particularly as part-time assistant teachers. With this experience I became fascinated with the wide differences between children of similar ages. All my former reading on ages and stages had led me to believe that young children had similar characteristics at specific ages. Now my preschool experiences showed me that, not only were there wide differences in their physical make-up, but also in their personalities, temperament and especially in the ways they learned new skills.

A visitor once commented on our own three children who were strikingly different. *Your kids look like you went to an international orphanage and said: I'll take that Irish boy over there with his reddish hair and all the freckles—that one creating his own music by plucking the rubber bands he stretched over the chair. Then I'll take that blonde Dutch girl with the pigtails—that one seeing how high she can jump on the bed. And I'll take that one over there who is chalk scribbling on the sidewalk—the French one with the brown eyes and brown curly hair.*

They certainly did have different learning patterns. Jerry talked early and fluently, probably because I had no one else to talk to when John was gone so much during the war. Cindy ignored my attempts at conversation until she was past two. At dinner time one evening I offered her mashed potatoes. Her answer was a loud and clear, *HELL NO !* Like a cork out of a bottle, from then on she talked constantly, day and night. Her new tricycle stayed in the garage for a year. One day she climbed on it and rode full speed around the block. We gave her private swimming lessons. She took a shower, but refused to even put a toe in the pool. When those lessons were over we took our family to a public pool with masses of splashing children. Within a week Cindy was jumping in the deep water and swimming like a fish. She seemed to mentally rehearse each new skill until she was ready to do it.

In the second year of our own valley preschool one of our school families attended a large family reunion in the San Francisco bay area. The following day they learned that a young cousin who had attended their gathering had been suddenly hospitalized with polio. We asked for advice from our county health department. Should the children who had been exposed to polio at the reunion be temporarily excluded from school? The health department told us that there was no reason to do so because it was not known how polio was spread.

We followed their advice, but within days the exposed children now had polio. Now should we close the school? The health officers said that such action would lead to panic in the whole community. Ignoring their recommendation, we did close the school, but it was too late. The dreaded virus had already spread to a number of our families. The most seriously affected were the exhausted parents who acquired polio while caring for their ill children. One mother died, another was confined to a wheel chair for life, and a father acquired paralysis of some facial muscles.

Only one child was permanently affected. I had driven him and our Mimi, now three, to school one morning. He became ill at school, was sent home and was soon hospitalized. Mimi, thoroughly exposed, did develop symptoms so we sent our older children to stay with their grandparents in San Francisco until the danger was passed. Our doctor told us not to bring Mimi to the hospital until she showed definite signs of paralysis. Early one morning she called to me and asked to be turned over. Testing, I told her to do it herself, but it was soon evident that she could not. Her crisis passed, and gradually her strength returned. We were one of the lucky families. For months Mimi's upper back muscles seemed weak. She drooped when she was tired. We took her swimming every day and her back became stronger. Two years later polio vaccine was developed. The dreaded scourge was wiped out, at least in our own country.

One of our neighbor's goats delivered twins, but she only tolerated feeding one of them. The other hungry little kid was given to Jerry to raise with a bottle. He named his goat, Heidi. She played with our children, with our dogs, Pat and Clancy, and became one of the family. One day my visiting aunt was napping outside with a flowered sun hat to protect her face. Heidi approached her from the rear and quietly ate the flowers from Aunt Rose's hat while she slept.

As Heidi grew we marveled at how high she could jump. Unfortunately one of her favorite games was to leap from the slope above our chicken houses onto their metal roof. She then frolicked up and down their length with her hard little hooves drumming on the aluminum. The banging was so traumatic for our hens that many of the next eggs they laid had blood inside them. Eggs were our livelihood, so we reluctantly returned Heidi to our neighbor's flock of goats. Days later, when the children went to visit Heidi, they ran home sobbing hysterically, *HEIDI'S NOT THERE! THEY ATE HER!*

For five years we raised chickens, apricots, giant zucchini and children. With the arrival of our fourth child, John Michael, whose name was soon shortened to Mike, our family was complete. Each child now had at least one brother and one sister. Mimi's bedroom was now Mike's nursery, so we moved Mimi upstairs with Cindy. Shortly after that a neighbor phoned to tell us she regularly watched out her window as Mimi would climb out the upstairs window to dance on the roof of the screen porch. We hesitated to nail the window shut in case of fire. So we discussed the danger with Mimi and hoped the practice would stop.

Then one warm afternoon when I was canning applesauce another rancher who lived two miles away phoned to say that Mimi was there. Apparently she locked Clancy in his pen so his red tail would not reveal her plans, then rode her tricycle away on this independent adventure. The neighbors found her sitting on the side of their swimming pool soaking her hot bare feet. We had moved to the country because we thought it would be safer for our children than city life, but now we began to wonder. We proved we could live in the country and survive, but the adventure was beginning to wear thin.

During our fifth year at the ranch there were a number of incidents to make us believe that the egg business was not the answer to our dreams. In mid July we had several days of over one hundred-degree temperature. Chickens cannot tolerate hot weather because their normal body temperature, like that of all birds, is unusually high. We had installed a sprinkler system in the chicken houses to cool the hens, but it was not enough this time. Both John and I sprayed the hens constantly with garden hoses. In spite of our spraying we lost over one hundred valuable laying hens.

One problem we did not anticipate with our chickens was what to do with the manure constantly accumulating under the cages. Three thousand hens, in addition to producing eggs, also produced over a ton of manure each week. We finally found another rancher with an orchard but no livestock to produce his own fertilizer for his trees. He brought his own truck to our ranch and a crew of his ranch hands. The odor was temporarily relieved each time they came.

This was not the only manure problem. An adult son of another neighbor died of a mysterious illness. Their ranch was farther down the slope than ours. They believed that we were responsible for their son's death. They claimed that our chicken manure had seeped into the soil, been washed downhill by rains and contaminated their well water which had then poisoned their son. It did not help our relationship with those neighbors when Mimi picked a bucket of berries from their bushes. Then our budding artist squashed the berries for paint and made a purple mural all over the side of their white house.

Another disaster was with our apricot trees. When we bought our ranch there were thirty of these mature trees. Each year the fruit ripened about the Fourth of July. We had a big picnic each year on that holiday, inviting our friends and relatives who would take home carloads of apricots. In our fifth year at the ranch a load of chicken feed we purchased was infested with earwigs. These hungry insects invaded our ripe apricots and the entire crop was lost.

Then came the turkey fiasco. As an experiment, and to vary our steady diet of chicken, we bought a dozen day-old turkeys. We read that turkeys are known to be severely retarded in intelligence. The report said that, if you put them in a square pen, one might accidentally get into a corner and, not smart enough to either turn around or back out, it would quickly die of dehydration. To avoid this possibility John cleverly improvised a round pen for our baby turkeys. One morning we found half of them dead. Apparently some unusual noise had spooked them and, like a European soccer catastrophe, they had piled on top of each other until the ones at the bottom were smothered.

When the six remaining turkeys were half grown we put them in a larger outdoor pen, anticipating that we would eat the largest Tom for our Thanksgiving dinner. One morning we found all six turkeys so severely injured that John had to complete the butchering process to put them out of their pain. Large dog prints in the soil and tufts of fluffy white fur on the scene were strong evidence that our neighbor's Samoyed dogs had jumped our fence in the night to attack the birds. We had turkey fryer meat in the freezer for months. The owner of the dogs reimbursed us for the loss, but it still seemed like one more in our series of catastrophes.

Another frustration we encountered was caused by the biological construction of hens. Like all birds, there is only one orifice for dropping both eggs and waste materials. Consequently, sometimes our eggs were soiled and had to be cleaned before we could sell them through our cooperative. Instructions from the agricultural extension service warned us not to wash soiled eggs because that would remove the natural invisible gelatinous protection over their shells. Then bacteria could be absorbed through the shells into the eggs. John built an electric buffer to remove the dried manure. Every evening we buffed and packed eggs on our back porch. Too often a thin-shelled egg, on touching the buffer, splattered all over the porch and all over us.

We were often introduced as the parents of one of our children who was involved in some escapade. *These are the parents of the boy who lost the school violin.* One afternoon Jerry briefly left his lunchbox and violin while waiting for the school bus. When he returned the violin was missing. He was not only sick with worry about the loss, but he was constantly embarrassed by teachers who chided him in front of other children about his carelessness. One week later the principal phoned to report that she had the violin. A teacher had picked it up at the bus stop and taken it to the office. They had cruelly kept it there as a lesson in responsibility for the whole school.

Toward the end of our fifth year as egg ranchers John came in the back door one afternoon and sat down with his head on his arms at the kitchen table. Lifting his face, he groaned, *I just put an end to Blackie with my bare hands. It was either him or me!* A number of wild domestic cats lived on our mountain. They shied away from human contact except in the spring when the females came down to our ranch to deliver their kittens. Fiercely protective of their young, they would only let us admire them from a distance. One mother cat left a pure black kitten behind when she led the rest of her brood back up the mountain. This one would spit at the children, but gradually he began to trust John who named him, Blackie. He never came close to our house, so we left food for him up at the pump house. This time, when John had gone into the pump house to check the well, Blackie leaped at his face in a genuine surprise attack. In self-defense John broke the cat's neck like one of the chickens until he was dead.

First we had to kill the boy chickens, then the extra puppies, then the puppies with the cleft palate. The neighbors ate our goat, Heidi, and the dogs killed our turkeys. Now it was Blackie, the cat. We needed to find a way to live without all the killing. We needed, instead, to celebrate life.

Most evenings a neighbor rancher, who was also the superintendent of the city schools, and his wife, exercised their horses on the road in front of our house. Our children usually ran out at these times to be lifted astride the horses and possibly get a short ride. Shortly after the Blackie incident the superintendent stopped one Spring evening with an interesting offer. His high school biology teacher had emergency surgery and would be on leave for the rest of the school year. Could John, with his college zoology major, take over? They would arrange for an emergency credential from the State. Our ranching days were over. We moved into town. The man who purchased our ranch apparently also became disenchanted with the egg business. He committed suicide by jumping off the Golden Gate Bridge.

BECOMING A TEACHER.

Like John, I also accidentally fell into the teaching business. Certainly in college I had never perceived myself in a teaching career. I was to live an exciting life as a war correspondent. One afternoon after we moved into town the telephone rang while I was reading to our preschooler, Mike. The other children were still at school. The caller identified himself as Bill, whom I remembered as a yell leader from our university days at Berkeley. Now Bill was an administrator in the office of our county schools.

Bill's soft pedal voice was a far cry from his days of arm waving and leading us in chanting and cheering for the Cal football team. He was seeking substitutes for the new special education classes in the valley. The State had not yet embarked on a training program for special education teachers, so a four-year college degree was the only requirement. He said that the students in these classes would not be able to learn anything academic. All the teachers would be expected to do was play games with them. He added that there was an urgent need for me to serve the community. Besides, my service hours might eventually help me get a real job in the field.

I reminded Bill that I had no desire to ever acquire a teaching credential. But, yes, I might be interested in taking the short course he offered for substitute training. I might gain invaluable information to improve my parenting skills and find out what our three older children were supposed to be learning at school. I enrolled Mike in an all-day preschool and took the course. It was a trap. In two weeks I was a teacher.

In spite of the current controversy in the courts over the validity of repressed memories, my clear recall of that first assignment is so vivid that I can play it over and over in my head like a horror movie. The regular teacher had been hospitalized for a *nervous condition*.

It was in early January and it had rained heavily the night before. The State Department of Education had assured the county schools office that, if they conducted special education classes for one year at their own expense, then the State would compensate them for similar classes in the following years. So the sites for these classes had been selected at minimal expense. Also, because the public might have some qualms about housing these new different children on existing school sites with regular children, first housing was based on selecting out-of-sight areas. The setting for my first experience was an ancient barn outside of town.

That first morning I parked my station wagon as close to the barn as I could, then walked across a rickety footbridge over a full running creek. No one else was in sight, so apparently I was in charge. I unlocked the squeaky barn door, then left it open until I found the switch to light three bulbs hanging on cords from the rafters. In the middle of the barn I saw an old gas heater with some matches lying near it. Lighting the gas flame, I noticed that there was no screen around this ancient appliance to prevent accidental burnings by young and possibly clumsy children.

The barn had been upgraded for use by a group of square dancers. A bathroom had been installed and a sink and hot plate served as their refreshment center. The only possible school materials in sight were some old magazines, a stack of books each labeled by a purple stamp, DIS-CARD, inside the cover, a gallon jar half full of school paste, a shoebox full of broken crayon pieces and a huge paper cutter. For school furniture there were two old kitchen-type tables, chairs in assorted sizes, and a lumpy couch covered with a flowered slipcover. Legs on the wobbly tables had been partially amputated to fit shorter people.

What would I be expected to do with these children who were due to arrive in thirty minutes? There were no directions in sight from the regular teacher. The substitute course had informed me that the teacher would always leave lesson plans to follow. Apparently her *nervous condition* had come on quickly. A small wave of panic washed over my recent breakfast. But Bill had assured me that being the mother of four young children and an active member of the coop preschool would be enough experience to handle it. Silently I called, INSTINCT, COME IN! I quickly tore pages out of the old magazines and cut them into strips with the paper cutter.

Spreading these strips over the tables, I then spooned big lumps of paste onto paper towels. At least this was a starting activity. We would make paper chains.

My students began to arrive, each one holding hands with a tired-looking, hovering mother. Bus service for these children had not yet been offered. Not one of the mothers asked who I was or why the regular teacher was not there. Apparently they were used to seeing substitute teachers. The children didn't even seem to know or care that a stranger had replaced their regular teacher. I wondered why they weren't more apprehensive. Had the personnel back at their institution changed so frequently that they were used to seeing new faces? All of these children had lived their entire lives at the State institution for the disabled until the State encouraged counties to establish special classes. Now these children could live at home and attend school.

By agreement with the State, the students were supposed to be from age 8 to 18, but my group was more spread. It was obvious the youngest boy could not be more than six, and the oldest boy, or rather young man, must be in his early twenties. These two had the facial characteristics of Downs Syndrome, with slightly slanted eyes.

Another very overweight boy, about ten, was wearing what we used to call coke bottle glasses. His eyes, magnified through the thick lenses, gave him the appearance of some creature from outer space. I was just about to ask him to stop bumping into the other children and knocking over chairs when I realized that he must be blind, or certainly with major visual impairment. I hoped he wouldn't bump into the gas heater and knock it over. He was not interested in the paper chain activity. Instead he settled into a corner on the floor, rocking himself forward and backward while making rhythmic, moaning sounds. The other children ignored him, so I did too.

Finding the class list in a drawer with the students' names, I made a name tag for each one to help me keep track. All of them, even the youngest, recognized their names and were delighted to identify themselves and let me pin on the tags. The two Downs students were Billy and Ralph. The sight-impaired youngster was George. There were five girls all seemingly around age nine or ten: Gina, Mary Lou, Audrey, Connie and Barbara. Four other boys looked to be a bit younger than the girls. Jimmy seemed to be the leader, then Robert, Peter and Sam.

Except for two, the entire group had light brown or blond hair and blue eyes. Jimmy had a shaggy carrot top. Gina's dark brown eyes were almost hidden with her long thick bangs. A shiny mane, almost black, covered her back and shoulders down to the wide sash at her waist.

The paper chain activity was even more successful than I had anticipated. Connie kept licking the paste from her fingers. Each of the other girls tried it, but didn't find it as tasty as Connie. There was an argument among them about the flavor, either like mashed potatoes or oatmeal. They finally agreed that it was most like the pudding they had when they lived at the hospital.

Their chains grew longer and longer as I cut up more and more magazines. By this time Billy's chosen activity was climbing on a chair and leaping on my back while yelling in my ear. One time he surprised me with his noisy game when I was using the paper cutter. Luckily I pulled my fingers away from this guillotine just in time. Each time I brought more paper strips to the table, Ralph, the tall Downs young man, reached out to rub the smooth surface of my nylon hose. Apparently his hormones were not impaired. The third time this happened I learned to keep a chair between us like a lion tamer in the circus. We recruited Ralph to hang our chains from some rusty old nails protruding from the barn rafters. Audrey squealed that we looked like a birthday party. So, to their delight, we sang *Happy Birthday to you* twelve times, once for each of the children.

At midmorning it was time to do something different with my twelve students. When I drove to the barn before school I saw what was probably their outdoor playground in the distance. Now a weak sun was shining through the clouds. Perhaps the playground was dry enough for us. We washed the paste from our hands and the girls busily scrubbed the sticky mess from the tabletops.

Putting on jackets, we all headed downhill across the footbridge over the creek. About a city block from the barn an area had been leveled for the playground where there were some swings and some monkey bars for climbing. The surface of the playground was dry, but was not covered with sand, pea gravel or wood chips commonly used for this purpose. Instead, it was covered with a thick layer of large rocks, each one as big as my fist. Now I understood why I had not seen any balls or jump ropes in the barn. They would need a smooth surface for play. Also, there was no fence to corral the children.

The girls quickly appropriated the swings. Ralph draped his long frame on the monkey bars while Billy climbed to the top. I wondered what I should do if he fell to the rocks below. The rest of the boys lined up at the edges of the playground area, picked up the rocks and had a contest to see who could throw them the farthest. There was nothing to damage in the surrounding muddy fields and no child left the perimeter to be a likely target so I left the boys alone.

All went well until Gina screamed and pointed. George had escaped! He was feeling his way by scruffing his shoes on a path and was half way to the busy highway about a block away. What to do? Should I leave the eleven and chase the one? Apparently this had happened before because all the children yelled at Ralph in chorus, as if rehearsed, *GO GET GEORGE!* Ralph untangled himself from the monkey bars and headed for George. His long arms and legs moved, uncoordinated, like a broken machine, but he was faster than George who couldn't see where he was going. We all cheered with relief when he took George by the hand and turned him around.

This was enough excitement for all of us, so I lined up my students to start back up the hill to the barn. Jimmy raced to the front of the line, yelling, *I'M THE LEADER,* and nobody argued. I positioned myself at the end of the line to prevent any more escapes. This time the climb was uphill. The children did stay on the path, even George. They periodically stopped beside the path along the way to gather new green weeds, which pulled up easily from the wet earth. The students and I were not in any hurry to get back to the barn. Now that the paper chain activity was over I kept wondering what I could do to keep these children busy for the rest of their school day. Could we make something with the weeds?

Jimmy was the answer to my dilemma. As the line leader he was the first to reach the footbridge over the creek. Common sense would tell any child that the rain-filled fast-running creek was dangerous. Apparently Jimmy was short on common sense because before I could stop him he climbed over the side-rail and jumped into the creek with a splash. As he lost his footing, the rushing water rapidly propelled him down stream toward me. Just in time I jumped into the water, grabbed his red hair and pulled him back to the bridge while the rest of the children clapped and cheered.

Fortunately no one decided to mimic Jimmy. Using my best in-charge voice I was able somehow to get us all back into the barn. The first order of business was to dry off a dripping boy who was cold and wet all over and a dripping teacher who was cold and wet to the waist. Placing a chair near the heater, I told Jimmy to sit there while I looked for something to dry us. I considered using the slipcover on the couch and then remembered the paper towels. We had used most of them for our paste activity. Perhaps there were more in the back of the storage closet. Bravely I ripped through a curtain of spider webs to the rear of the closet where I could see a large carton with a picture of paper towels on its side. Just as I picked up a package, the door was slammed shut. The lock clicked and I was in complete darkness with the spiders.

At first I heard the children cheering and laughing at their prank and assumed they would let me out. Wrong! Unmistakably there were sounds of water running. Someone had turned on the water in the sink and also in the bathroom basin. My ears told me the children were filling cups, having a water fight and splashing it around the room.

Occasionally there was a loud sizzle as the water hit the hot surface of the gas heater. In the total blackness, huddling against the door away from the spider webs, I could not tell if there might be a heavy object in the closet to use for smashing open the door. I tried it with my wet shoes, but that didn't even make enough noise to attract the children's attention. In their frenzied slipping and sliding I hoped they would not knock over the free standing heater with the open flame. Which would come first for me—to die from smoke inhalation or incineration? Being a war correspondent might have been a safer occupation than this teaching!

Bill was wrong. Nothing in my mothering or preschool experience had prepared me for this crisis. It was not quite noon and the parents would not come to retrieve their children until 2:00. My pleas to open the door were ignored. The children were having too good a time splashing the water around the room and sliding in the puddles. Somewhere in the far reaches of my brain a light was blinking. I recalled reading somewhere that one of the common characteristics of Downs individuals is very dry skin. Water left on their skin could result in severe, painful chapping. Hearing Billy's voice near the door, I called to him and reminded him that his wet hands would get very sore. I had the towels. My brain storm strategy worked. Billy unlocked the closet door and I escaped.

There was no longer a question about what would be our next activity. I sent Ralph into the closet to get some fresh paper towels. No way was I going in there again! I turned off all the faucets. All of us spent the next hour mopping up their flood with the paper towels and sweeping the water out the barn door while Jimmy dried off by the heater. The children quieted down for lunch. I read to them from the books labeled, DIS-CARD, while Billy took a nap on my lap. When the mothers returned I assured them that *all had gone well. No problem! The puddles outside the barn door were probably from another rain shower.* Jimmy's mother noticed that he seemed a bit damp, but said that he often perspired heavily.

I needed to try to relax before I went home to change roles and become a mother, so I lay down on the old couch. Most of the magazines had been cut up for chains. But I needed something to read to turn off the morning's images in my head. Above the couch on a high shelf the regular teacher had lined up a group of professional books. Selecting one with the title, *Hygiene for the Retarded,* I skimmed though it and found this suggestion, *If you have a child with a pointed head, never part his hair in the middle.* Laughing aloud at this advice until the tears came, I soon fell asleep exhausted.

Later, at home, I began to reflect on the day's events. I phoned the hospitalized regular teacher for advice. She suggested that the only way to survive in the job was to keep a sense of humor. *Laugh at the children,* she said. Apparently this attitude had not been enough for her. And so far I had not experienced anything funny except for the hygiene book.

Certainly the county schools office needed to know that this special class was not safe for either the students or the teacher. It was my civic duty to let them know. The superintendent phoned to ask me to continue subbing while the regular teacher was hospitalized. I told him about the free standing gas heater with the open flame, the rocky rough surface of the playground, the full running creek and the guillotine paper cutter with no guard to protect fingers. I added that, simply as a concerned citizen, I believed that the school site was unsafe for any children, let alone these retarded ones.

Knowing that I did not have a teaching credential, his reply to me, *THAT IS ONLY YOUR LAY OPINION,* was like a red flag before an angry bull. Never before had I been interested in owning a credential. But at that exact moment his message reached my ears I vowed to somehow acquire that piece of paper. Some day then I could voice not a lay opinion, but a professional opinion.

To get more experience, I substituted in those difficult special classes for three years. It was almost a full time job because all the teachers needed frequent time out periods to recuperate from the stress of unsafe conditions and inadequate materials to serve the children with their varied needs. In the second year when the State began to fund the classes as they promised, the only evident changes were a screen around the gas heater and smooth surfacing and a fence for the playground. Bus service for the children was offered. At my urging the lock for the storage closet was removed.

The legal selection process for assignment of children to these classes was not yet in gear. Principals of the regular schools were allowed free rein to move any students into the special classes who did not meet their particular whims or qualifications. One principal sent all six children from one family. These children needed a bath and clean clothes, but none of them seemed retarded or with any particular disability. Their mother was a microcephalic whose scalp bones had fused at birth, leaving her with an infant sized head and brain, but fully developed reproductive organs. She could produce children, but not care for them. These children simply had no home stimulation to encourage social or mental growth to prepare them for school. I bought shampoo for head lice. Each of the six regularly climbed on a stool at the school's sink to be deloused before their problem spread to the other children, and to me.

Larry was about seven when he was added to one of these classes. He was obviously not retarded or physically impaired. But Larry needed full time supervision because he was so full of anger that he constantly injured other children. His mother had deserted him and he was in foster care. His deep need for mothering was evident. Every time a teacher would sit down Larry would cry and climb on her lap to be held.

Most women teachers in those days were still wearing dresses and shoes with heels. By this time, however, with the need to move quickly to avoid disaster I had learned to bring a pair of tennis shoes. One day my students were all settled down for lunch. I noticed that Larry was in a corner eating quietly by himself, so I slipped into an adjoining area to get some paint for the afternoon activity. A loud protest, *NO! NO! MINE!* From one of the other children let me know that Larry was at it again. His back was toward me so he did not see or hear me return with my soft-soled shoes. I reached over his head to hold his hand clutching the other child's sack of cookies.

Returning them to the owner, I led Larry back to his own lunch while he wailed, *YOU AND YOUR GODDAM SNEAKY SHOES!*

Then there was Harold. He had receptive language, but no expressive language. He could understand directions and made some voice noises, but he had never spoken any understandable words. At the end of each school day we made separate lines of students waiting outside for each bus. There was another line for children whose parents would pick them up. I had not noticed that Harold was in the wrong line. When his group surged forward to enter a bus Harold let out a hair-raising protest, *I DON'T RIDE THE BUS! MY MOM GETS ME!* Larry left his bus line and pushed Harold to the ground yelling, *YOU FOOLED US! YOU CAN TALK!* I rescued Harold and held his hand until his mother drove up. I told her what had happened, but she didn't believe it. And Harold never talked again

In my second year in the special classes Tom joined the group. He was not yet the minimum eight years old, but the administration stretched the rules to accommodate his family. Pediatricians had classified Tom as retarded all his short life until his seven-year-old check up when they discovered that he was profoundly deaf.

Tom had no group experiences with other children until he joined us. Even other children in his neighborhood had not been allowed to play with him for fear he would hurt them. For his first week Tom sat on the sidelines watching the other children. He shook his head when we tried to get him to join in our activities. The second week he exploded into frenetic movement as if now he had figured out that he was expected to be part of the class.

Tom was large for his age and exceptionally strong and well-coordinated in contrast to the rest of the children. At first his favorite activity was to chase one of the children like an untrained puppy and push the child to the ground. He didn't seem to understand that he was responsible for hurting the others. The mothers of the other children were beginning to protest and I didn't have any answers. One morning I sat everybody down for their circle time where we sang, did finger plays in rhyme or read a short story. While I had the children's attention we discussed our problem with Tom. They were pointing out skinned knees and other injured body parts.

Then Gina blurted out, *I KNOW! IF WE DON'T RUN AWAY FROM TOM, THEN HE WILL STOP CHASING US!* This amazingly logical solution was the answer. I began to wonder if some of these children, like Gina, were really retarded. The children stopped running from Tom and his rough game came to an end.

Because his deafness had not been discovered until late in his short life, Tom had not learned to communicate with signing, lip reading, or what the deaf community called oralism, an attempt at meaningful voice noises. When I shook my head at him he did understand it meant, NO. And when I bobbed my head up and down with a smile on my face he understood that I was approving of his activity.

Tom's favorite activity was drawing, at which he seemed particularly gifted. He was able to make some objects smaller in his pictures to indicate distance. His pictures conveyed messages to us at sharing times. Tom also spent part of every morning poring over the tattered books in our meager library corner. One of his favorite books was a child's dictionary where each picture had a word beside it. One day at sharing time he showed a picture of a boy he had drawn looking much like a self portrait and pointed to himself. Beside it he had copied from his dictionary the word, BOY. I told the children the meaning of the word and they loudly clapped and cheered for Tom.

I enrolled in an evening course in signing for the deaf to help me communicate with Tom, but he couldn't understand why I was waving my hands and fingers at him. Then I ordered a chart of the signed alphabet I found in a catalog of teacher materials. Each letter had a picture of the hand sign which represented it. I made a set of name tags so all the children could use them for matching their letters to the hand signs. With his short name, Tom was the first to learn how to sign his name. Then he insisted on teaching one child at a time to do so until all the children could play this game except for our visually handicapped George.

During the rest of that school year Tom spent more and more time copying words from the picture dictionary and labeling his drawings with them. One morning he bounced into the classroom, the first child to arrive. Excitedly he made some loud noises and pointed to his shiny new shoes. He spent the first hour at the drawing table carefully making another self-portrait. Occasionally he would go to our floor length mirror to check out the clothes he was wearing to add them to his picture. Then he took the dictionary and labeled his picture carefully, TOM BROWN SHOES. Overwhelmed with emotion at his amazing accomplishment, tears came to my eyes and I hugged him and then kept bobbing my head up and down to show my pleasure. He bobbed his head up and down with a big grin on his face and pointed again to his new shoes.

One day I wondered again why Gina had been labeled retarded though she had been enrolled at what they called, *the home*, near her second birthday. She brought the book titled, *Spotty*, to me which the children had asked me to read to them over and over. The story was about a rabbit who was born with spots when the rest of his brothers and sisters were plain white. Spotty was teased about his difference until he ran away and found a family of spotted rabbits just like him. Pointing to Spotty on the book's cover, Gina observed, *Spotty is like Tom. What if they didn't let Tom come to our school just because he couldn't talk to us?*

Tom only spent one school year with us. As soon as he was eight he was eligible to attend the state boarding school for the deaf where he could learn other ways to communicate besides his pictures. He seemed so young to have to live away from his family. We had a good-bye party for him on his last day. I hugged him and reflected on this amazing child who had once been labeled retarded.

Jenny came to us in my last year with the special education classes. She had been a premature baby who had been blinded by too much administered oxygen to assist her undeveloped lungs in her first days after birth.

She was one of the last babies afflicted with what was called retrolental fibroplasia before the medical profession discovered what was causing the blindness of preemies. Our schools had not yet offered classes for the blind or visually handicapped, so Jenny joined our special education group.

Like Tom, she was a constant surprise in how she had compensated for her impairment. On her first day I took her hand and showed her the activities from which she could choose. I deliberately avoided painting, drawing and writing, assuming these would require sight. To my surprise the drawing area became one of her favorite activities. With Jenny's super-sensitive fingertips she could feel the raised waxy lines she made with her crayons. She had no sight to differentiate between the colors of crayons. Apparently, however, they seemed to have different levels of warmth to her fingers depending upon the chemical composition of their pigments. She could distinguish purple by its cool feel to her fingers. But the warmth of orange was her favorite.

When the playground was surfaced Jenny was one of the most adept of our group in jumping rope. She had no fear of the twirling rope she could not see. Her sensitive ears could pick up the sound of the rope as it touched the ground telling her when to jump. She rarely missed. One day on the way home I passed Jenny's house. She was skating fearlessly on the sidewalk with other neighbor children.

Like Tom, Jenny also had a strong interest in alphabet letters. She would run her fingertips over the contour of our wooden letters and ask for the speech sound or alphabet name for a letter that interested her. Sometimes she liked to roll clay into what she called snakes or worms, then form letters with them. One morning she called me to show that she had tried to compose her name with the wooden letters, GANE. So I showed her how to spell it correctly, JENNY. Later, when our schools offered classes for the blind, Jenny learned to write in the Braille system a year and a half sooner than normal expectation. Her instructor said that she believed Jenny's first exploration with our alphabet letters had laid the mental foundation for the more difficult and abstract Braille.

One would assume that both the senses of sight and hearing are necessary for success in early literacy. Yet Tom was deaf and Jenny was blind. He had sight but no language. She had language but no sight. These two had stronger interest in learning to read and write than any of the other special education students with intact senses. Was it their drive to overcome their impairments? Was it because they were both unusually physically coordinated? Both their gross and fine motor development were superior. Could that be one of the missing links to literacy? Most beginning reading programs at that time simply expected young students to look and listen.. But Tom couldn't listen and Jenny couldn't look.

Wooden Valley

Apparently my outburst after my first day as a substitute teacher in special education had not prejudiced the superintendent against me. He called me to his office one summer day at the end of my third year of service. He asked me to interview for a position at the one-room rural Wooden Valley School in a small community on the other side of the mountain from Napa Valley. I would be teaching regular children, not those with special needs.

My lack of a credential did not seem to matter to him. *The State will issue you an emergency credential. You won't need to take any courses beyond your university degree.* He held out a carrot in front of my nose. *If you teach at Wooden Valley for two years, then the State will grant you a full teaching credential. The State assumes that experience will substitute for college courses.* Did the State really believe that on the job learning by doing was more valuable than studying the Education field with books and taking college classes? Realistically, there was a major teacher shortage at that time and there were not enough credentialed teachers to fill the need. At least this offer couldn't be more dangerous and stressful than substituting in the special classes. It didn't take long for me to make up my mind.

At my interview the president of the Wooden Valley school board outlined their expectations of me. *There are only eighteen students, about the same age spread as your own children at home. Your ranch experience will help you understand the interests of rural children. We're not particularly concerned about what you should teach them. They hated their last three teachers. So your biggest task will be to change our children's attitudes so they will like school again.*

They gave me the keys to the school. So one Sunday afternoon our whole family drove out to check the site for mother's new job. To get there it was a thirty-minute ride over a narrow, curving, steep mountain road. The school building, beside a quiet country road with little traffic, was only two years old. The county schools office had recommended that Wooden Valley close their ancient run-down school several years before. They suggested that these ranchers should unite with another small school in a valley to the north, but their recommendation had been voted down. Instead, the Wooden Valley residents had insisted on building their own new school.

The original old weathered wooden building had been bulldozed aside and was leaning over the side of a creek running in front of the school. It must have been built for the children of families who crossed the country in covered wagons perhaps before California became a state in the middle of the nineteenth century. It seemed disrespectful just to leave it there like something dead after all those years of service to children in this valley.

The new school was a sturdy building made of cement blocks, tan with a hint of pink. Three of the walls were solid brick. One wall had a row of windows overlooking the playground area. The interior was divided into an ample front hall with two bathrooms at one end, a storage room that ran the whole length of one inside wall, and the central large classroom. Book shelves under the windows held grade level books for all six grades. Radiant heating was supplied with pipes embedded in the cement floor. The full running creek in front would be handy for nature study projects. The school board had informed me that janitor service would be supplied at the end of each day by a parent of one of the students.

The trustees admonished me that both doors to the storage room must be locked at all times. They called it, Fort Knox. I assumed that there must be something of great value or great secrecy stored there. Unlocking both doors, I found a light switch and warned our children not to touch anything in the valuable contents.

Inside we found the dishes and coffeepot no doubt used for the mothers' club meetings. With them was a red satin handkerchief box to pass around for donations to cover the coffee expense. Another shelf was filled with old maps. Jerry, our eldest, suggested that some of them must have been used when people still thought the world was flat. Two shelves had old textbooks for seventh and eighth grades, though these grade level students now went by bus to junior high in town. Mimi insisted that one of the old books probably had a treasure map inside. Cindy found a small box of basaltic arrowheads probably left behind by the Indians who once lived in Wooden Valley. No doubt they were found by some schoolboy hunting rabbits and brought to school. We found a non-functioning movie projector, a broken phonograph and several tattered American flags. John used a short stepladder to check the contents of a box on the topmost shelf. In it were attendance records going back seventeen years. Maybe they were important and needed to be kept in a safe place. I locked both doors again for Fort Knox and we headed back home over the mountain. All the family agreed that this job was going to be much more pleasant than the special education classes.

We spent the rest of the summer relaxing and anticipating school opening in September. The six of us would each be attending a different school. Mike was starting kindergarten at one elementary school. Mimi would be in fourth grade at another. Cindy would be in one junior high and John would be teaching in another. Jerry would be in high school, and I would be at Wooden Valley.

School opening was the Monday after Labor Day, so I headed over the mountain named, George. The early morning sun had not reached the west side of the slope as I drove through the typical mid-California landscape of oak, buckeye and madrone forest. The poison oak vines beside the road were beginning to warn, DON'T TOUCH, as their green leaves were turning to red. A doe and her fawn leaped across the road in front of me. This morning ride, with nature's feast, was going to be a refreshing way to start each school day. The top of the mountain turned into pine forest. Part way down the other side I was stopped by a red-coated flag-man from the road department. Heavy equipment was widening the road.

While I was impatiently waiting I told the flagman that, as the new teacher for Wooden Valley, I would be driving this road every day. Frowning, he warned me, *If you're going to be in charge of all those kids, you'd better get a snakebite kit. This roadwork will be going on for months. The rattlers have been driven from their holes by this construction. They're crawling all over the place.*

My plan was to arrive early for any last preparations before the children would show up, but the unexpected delay by the roadwork on the mountain had altered my plan. Three students were already waiting at the door. The largest child introduced two siblings. *We're all from the Clark ranch. You can see our barn, up the road a piece.* I could see the big red barn in the distance. *I'm Lil. This is my brother, Benny. He's in second. Katy, here, is in first. She's never been to school yet. Our brother, Gilman, waited for the bus. He's in fifth.*

As we unlocked the door I asked Lil, *Do you ever get snakes on the play-ground?* Lil grinned, guessing my concern. *Oh, sure! But I'll show you where we keep the snakebite kit. Do you have the keys to Fort Knox?* I unlocked the double doors and Lil brought out a box with a red cross on it labeled, FIRST AID. Unfolding the directions for snakebite, I read, *First make parallel cuts in the area around the wound with the razor blade.* No one had told me that I had to be the paramedic as well as being the teacher!

A small yellow school bus full of children arrived. They were seemingly all in uniform, blue jeans and tee shirts. Some wore new cowboy boots. Except for two girls with long braids, all their hair was about the same length. I would have to sort out the boys from the girls when I matched them up with their names on the list. I asked the bus driver if it was safe to let the children play outside with so many snakes around. He laughed at me. *You must be city folks. These kids know enough to jump over the snakes.*

I told the children to put their lunches inside the building and then go out to the playground until it was time for school. I stayed on the cement porch at the front of the building where I could watch the play. Somebody had to be near the telephone in case of an emergency. Mentally I reviewed the snake bite directions. *First make parallel cuts around the wound with the razor blade.*

A large black truck with three small boys in the back bed came to a noisy stop in front of the school. The largest of the three pushed the other two to the floor of the truck bed, vaulted over the side rail, stomped the dust from his boots, waived to the driver, and slowly came up to me on the porch and refused my outstretched hand. *Are you the new teacher?* I assured him that I was. Then he stuck out his chin. *I'm Johnny. I'm in first grade.*

I'M NOT GOING TO LEARN TO READ,
AND YOU CAN'T MAKE ME DO IT!

I counted heads on the playground and realized that Johnny was the eighteenth, the last to arrive. The county superintendent had told me not to start school until 9:00, so we still had ten minutes before our official opening. There were no more students to greet, so I sat down on the cement steps already warmed by the September sun where I could watch the playground. In spite of his belligerent announcement Johnny did not seem to regard me as the enemy. He sat down beside me. *My brothers get to ride in the truck with my dad today. I'm the oldest, so I have to go to school. I'm in first grade.* Then he straightened his shoulders and loudly repeated his threat,

I'M NOT GOING TO LEARN TO READ,
AND YOU CAN'T MAKE ME DO IT!

Ignoring the subject, I asked Johnny about the old wooden building leaning over the creek on the opposite side from the playground. *Oh that's the old school. That's where my dad went when he was a kid. They pushed it out of the way to make room for this new school.* I wondered what it would have been like teaching in that rickety old wooden building instead of this new sturdy school made of pink cement blocks. It probably had a pot-bellied stove instead of the warmed floors of our new school.

Shivers went up and down my back as Johnny dragged his long fingernails through the rough grout between the cement blocks on the porch. I volunteered to cut his nails, but he growled, *NAH! I'M SHARPENING THEM TO POINTS SO I CAN SCRATCH MY LITTLE BROTHERS UNTIL THEY BLEED.* His face softened a bit. *They get to ride in the truck today, but I have to go to school.*

At 9:00 I let Johnny shake the ancient brass hand-held school bell. The students with fresh haircuts and new shoes spontaneously lined up by size, eighteen in all, with Johnny, the smallest as the leader. Some of the children had faster growing rates over the summer. So their places in line had to be rearranged. After introducing myself again I asked them to walk inside and find a desk in their own size. Definite seating would be decided later as we became acquainted. No one had reported seeing a rattlesnake. Maybe this wouldn't be so scary after all.

Mentally rehearsing my speech of welcome, my eyes swept across the playground to check once more for snakes. I noticed movement in the trees separating the school property from the vineyards. More bodies in assorted sizes were racing toward the school. As they came closer I counted eighteen more children. These were dark-haired with tan skin so they must belong to the farm workers, the seasonal fruit and grape pickers. These migrants, of Mexican heritage, travel with their families following the crops to be harvested. The new children shyly stared at me standing on the porch. The largest one, a girl, whispered, *Escuela?* My mouth opened and closed a few times while I was mentally dusting off my high school Spanish. Then finally something came out resembling, *Si! Buenos Días. Ven.*

The school board had not mentioned this possibility. Instantly I had become not only a one-room school teacher, but a bilingual teacher as well, and of thirty-six children, not eighteen. At the rear of the classroom were some long low tables and benches, which I had planned to use for special activity centers. I motioned to the new ones to follow me and *Sientense aqui.* Miraculously the eighteen newcomers understood my Spanish and slid onto the benches waiting and watching me for further directions. When I managed to blurt out, *Como se llama,* the oldest girl, who seemed to be in charge, responded, *Marta.* Then she named the others. I gave them paper, pencils and a box of broken crayons from the store room, then went back to try to sort out the original students..

We spent the next hour and a half passing out grade level books and workbooks according to numbers and names on the list, fitting the resident children to desks, and beginning to cluster age groups together. I placed the four first graders near my desk at the front of the room. When I gave a preprimer to Johnny he handed it back to me, loudly repeating again,

I'M NOT GOING TO LEARN TO READ, AND YOU CAN'T MAKE ME DO IT!

The other three little first graders ignored him and turned the pages of their books, looking at pictures. More of my Spanish was beginning to return. At mid-morning I managed, *VAMOS AFUERA,* and we all went outside for a long recess. Lil was accepted by all as the leader and invited the migrant children to join in their baseball game. Their lack of English was no handicap. Apparently both sets of children mingled each year at harvest time and had learned to communicate with each other. Everyone seemed to know the baseball rules, so I was only the spectator. But I kept my eye out for snakes.

Returning to our classroom after recess I noticed Lil going into the boys' bathroom. With that name and a headful of golden blond curls I had assumed Lil was a girl. Quickly checking my official list again, I found, *Lilburn,* not *Lillian.* Lil was a boy!

I wrote a reading and a workbook assignment for each grade level on the chalkboard in front of the room. Interested in their new materials, all the students went uncomplainingly to work, leaving me free to work with the four youngest, the non-readers. It was their first school experience because the rural schools did not offer kindergarten. To begin to assess what they knew I gave each of them a small chalkboard and a piece of chalk. None of them could write his or her name. At least that was a place to start. Johnny did show some interest in making J and O letters on his chalkboard. He put faces inside his O's and legs on them to turn them into people. It was apparent that Johnny liked to draw.

At noon the migrant children slipped out and disappeared into the vineyards. They did not return until the following morning. Lil showed me the lunch routine. The students carried their lunch boxes outside to the picnic tables, then after lunch they went back to baseball. Without the migrants they needed all the children to make up two teams. They divided themselves fairly by size with two first graders on each team. The bigger children helped the little ones bat, then held their hands to run around the bases. The sensitivity and cooperation of these rural children was most surprising to observe compared to the competitive me-first attitude I had assumed was normal in city children. Could it be that having siblings and mixed-age students in the same class was an advantage?

Back in the classroom after lunch recess I described my own family to the students: My husband, John, a science teacher and former rancher, Jerry, our oldest child, Cindy and Mimi in between, and Mike who had just started kindergarten back in town. Giving each student a new box of crayons from the store room, I requested that they draw a picture of their own family. Only one child resisted the task. Mitchell, a handsome, large sixth grader with curly black hair, complained, *I CAN'T DRAW!* Then, noticing that the others were busily drawing, he finally produced a primitive group of three stick figures all the same size.

In Johnny's picture the dominant figure was a large man in the center in a cowboy hat. In a line on one side of the man Johnny drew his smaller mother. On the other side were three little boys in a row, each one smaller than the other, like one of those Russian toys with each smaller doll fitting inside the larger one.

When I invited the students to share their drawings with the group I began to understand why Mitchell was so resistant. Hiding his drawing behind his back, he announced, *My mom and dad don't live with me and I don't have any brothers or sisters. I live with my grandma and grandpa. They are very old.* Mitchell was obviously embarrassed about his different home life from the other students. When all the children had introduced their families with their pictures I mounted them on a bulletin board which I labeled, OUR FAMILIES. We clustered each drawing under its family name heading. There were eight local families in attendance. In addition to the four Clarks, we had three Jones, two Parkers, one Cleveland, one Durbin, two Wests, two Browns and three named Martinez. At least Mitchell had the same name as his grandparents, so he didn't have to feel different about that.

To end our first day I clustered all the children on the floor, sat in a low chair near them, and read aloud the first chapter from Swiss Family Robinson. Johnny fell asleep with his head in Katy's lap and Lil carried him to the school bus. I had survived the first day. No rattlesnakes had appeared. I had remembered some of my Spanish. No one had locked me in the storeroom. No one had jumped into the creek beside the school. Yes, this was going to be easier than substituting in the special classes.

Using the reading books and workbooks for each level, which had been ordered by the school board, we soon had a schedule worked out for the eighteen resident students: Reading and Math in the mornings, Social Studies on Monday and Tuesday afternoons, Science on Wednesday and Thursday afternoons, and Spelling on Friday. Before too many days passed it became obvious, however, that these grade level materials did not match most of the students' levels of reading. By having each child read a short passage from different grade level books I determined that most of them were trying to read books which were about a grade level above their achievement levels. It was frustrating for them and for me.

Working down level by level I tried to assess a reading level for Mitchell who had been assigned to sixth grade. After he read a few pages aloud to me in a fourth grade book I stopped him and asked a few questions about the content to see if he understood what he had been reading. Unable to answer correctly, he blurted out, *THAT'S NOT FAIR! YOU DIDN'T TELL ME TO LISTEN!* Obviously Mitchell thought that reading was simply regurgitating the printed words on the page. He had no mental images for recall of the content. No wonder he couldn't do the assignments in his sixth grade workbook.

I wondered what had been lacking in Mitchell's background. His family drawing with stick figures had been the least mature of all the students, even the first graders. Should we add a daily drawing time to help build visual images for reading comprehension? What else?

Trying to recall what in my own background had fostered visualization, I remembered that as a child when I regularly listened to the Lone Ranger on our radio, I had vivid mind pictures of his adventures with his Indian friend, Tonto. Had television, supplying images for children, robbed them of the ability to make their own mind pictures when reading? Was there a way to recapture it? Perhaps reading to the children every day from books without pictures as I was already doing at the end of each school day might help.

Now I understood why these children hated school. They needed assignments where they could be successful. No one likes to be constantly reminded of his or her inadequacies. The two older Clark boys, Lil and Gilman, were the only students who could read their assigned books without help. Apparently these two had better teaching in their first school years than the younger children. No wonder the school board said the children disliked their last two teachers.

The migrants came every morning. At reading time Marta kept them in their special area at the back of the room. Since we had no extra materials for them they quietly kept busy with puzzles, board games and looking at books from our small class library. One of their favorite activities was drawing, but our supply of paper was dwindling. Their drawing skill seemed far superior to the resident children's work. I wondered what in their culture had fostered this ability.

Sometimes they would look at pictures in the books and make up stories in Spanish. I noticed that Marta was particularly skilled in this story-making activity. First she would tell a story to her little ones, turning the pages of a book to show the pictures. Later they would pick up the same book and tell stories to each other. I wished I could give them more help, but I was hired to teach the other resident students. They needed a lot of help too.

Fortunately Marta kept the migrants in their area, freeing me to supervise the others. None of the four first graders had been exposed to a kindergarten so their skills were too immature to carry on many independent activities. One morning Johnny noticed that the migrants were having a finger painting session under Marta's guidance, so he joined them and the other three first graders followed. Marta became my invaluable aide for these four. In the back of my mind, however, I knew that somehow it was my responsibility to teach them to read before June, even reluctant Johnny.

Math symbols represent the same quantities in both English and Spanish. Only the names for the numerals are different. So the migrants could do math with us. All thirty-six students learned to count to one hundred in both languages. By pairing off the two sets of students at math time, one resident and one migrant, they shared the books and helped each other with the problems. We needed paper for math for thirty-six students instead of eighteen.

The first graders counted on their fingers in both English and Spanish. Shy Juanito became a close friend to Johnny when Marta explained to him that they had the same name with a slight difference in pronunciation. These two sat together at math time, waving fingers and translating for each other. The language exchange was mutual, neither taking the lead:

CINCO DEDOS…FIVE FINGERS
CUATRO DEDOS…FOUR FINGERS
CINCO DEDOS Y CUATRO DEDOS SON NUEVE DEDOS.
FIVE FINGERS AND FOUR FINGERS ARE NINE FINGERS.

Sometimes it came out in Spanglish.

FIVE DEDOS AND FOUR DEDOS ARE NINE DEDOS.

One morning Juanito and Johnny took off their shoes and counted their toes in both Spanish and English.

In our third week of school I attended the evening meeting of the local school board at their invitation. When they asked if I had any problems I first requested materials for the migrant children. And what should I do about the shrinking paper supply? Lilburn Clark, Senior, the president of the board, told me not to give the migrants any more school paper. I should just keep them busy because they would move away in six weeks after the harvest. And there would be no new supplies for any students for the rest of the school year.

I tried to explain that most of the materials which had been ordered for reading did not match the students' needs, except for the two older Clark boys. Gilman was such a good reader that he would probably benefit from more of a challenge. He was always the first one to finish his assignment. Then he bothered the others until I found something for him to do. I asked permission to reassign books so that children would be less frustrated, or bored like Gilman.

All the board members loudly disagreed with me. If I gave Gilman the same assignment as his brother, there might be a problem at home. They insisted that the major problem was simply that their children had disliked their former teachers. Mr. Clark repeated that my main job was to change the students' attitude and make school a happy place to be but still use the assigned grade level materials.

How could I change children's attitudes toward school when they were constantly frustrated with materials which were too difficult for them? At home, during a restless night, I came up with a possible solution. The next morning I was ready to experiment. I tied a red bandana on a yardstick for my magic wand, touched each child on the shoulder with it, and turned all the resident students, except the first graders, into teachers. Every student was assigned to another student one grade below. At reading time these new teachers helped their assigned individual students. They read aloud the directions in the workbooks and they all helped figure out new words. Three of the partner pairs were siblings whose respectful caring for each other was gratifying to see. No sibling problem here. All students had an opportunity to practice reading where they could be successful, one grade level below their assigned books. That left me free to figure out a way to begin to teach the non-readers, our four first graders. Johnny still loudly repeated every day.

I'M NOT GOING TO LEARN TO READ,
AND YOU CAN'T MAKE ME DO IT!

He did cooperate, however, when we worked on our individual chalkboards. He had learned to write his name, John, though sometimes it came out, *Jonh.* He had noticed that one of the letters was taller than the other, but he just couldn't remember which one comes first, the short one or the tall one. He resisted looking at books, but he participated enthusiastically in all our drawing activities. He seemed to be a doer, not a looker or a listener.

Except for the one wall with windows, the other three classroom walls were covered with chalkboards. At math time we squeezed as many pairs of students as could fit at the boards to save paper. To augment our supply of drawing and craft materials I began to frequent the piles of throw away materials at the rear of shopping areas in town, like a homeless bag lady. The creative migrant children showed the resident students how to make collages and sculptures out of fruit box liners and small box parts. In the back of one market I found a box full of purple tissue paper squares for wrapping apples. Under the tutelage of the migrants all the children fashioned purple butterflies. Their bodies were strips of fruit box liners rolled into tubes and brightly painted. We hung their butterflies from the ceiling so they would flutter in moving air. There was little breeze, however, in our warm Fall days.

A county school nurse spent a day with us for basic check-ups for vision and hearing. All the children, even the migrants, were found to have intact senses. The nurse kindly told me to ignore the scary directions for snakebite. Instead, in case this happened, I should phone a family living near the school, assign one of the older students to be in charge, put the bitten child in my station wagon and head for the hospital in town.

Barring delay with the roadwork, I could probably get to the hospital safely in half an hour. At least I wouldn't have to make those bloody cuts around a bite.

The business manager from the county schools office came one afternoon to give me directions for keeping attendance according to state law. He told me to sign these forms with the title, TEACHER-PRINCIPAL. My career was progressing rapidly in spite of no credential. I not only was a bilingual teacher, now I was a principal! He said these legal forms must be kept forever. So that's why there were seventeen years of them in Fort Knox!

Just as I first assumed, the creek was invaluable for nature study. Johnny came running to me one morning recess carrying a small turtle he had found in the creek. I remembered seeing a glass terrarium in Fort Knox. The first graders made a home for the turtle using small plants and rocks from the creek. Now we had a science project as well as a class pet. Because he had found it, Johnny was voted to name it, Tim Turtle.

After school I went to the public library in town for books about turtles. The next day Gilman, reading one of the books, yelled out, *OUR TURTLE CAN'T BE NAMED, TIM. IT'S A GIRL!* Assuming there would be some simple explanation for turtle sexes, such as colorations for birds, I asked Gilman to share his discovery. He stood up and held out both his hands, palms down, with the fingers curled under. Extending one hand, he said, *THIS ONE IS THE GIRL TURTLE.* Then he placed his other curved hand on top of the first one. *THIS IS THE BOY TURTLE MATING WITH THE GIRL.* As all the students were reared on local ranches with livestock they were aware of the sex life of animals and accepted Gilman's explanation as matter of fact information. No one giggled. Then Gilman turned his boy hand over, demonstrating its concave curve. *SEE—BOY TURTLES ARE CURVED ON THEIR BOTTOM SHELL SO THEY FIT WHEN THEY MOUNT THE GIRLS. GIRL TURTLES HAVE BOTTOM SHELLS THAT ARE FLAT. TIM'S SHELL IS FLAT, SO IT HAS TO BE A GIRL.* Tim was renamed, Tilly.

Driving home that afternoon, I finally figured out a possible way to encourage Johnny to learn to read without his realizing that it was happening. Using his interest and skill in drawing, perhaps we could use the draw-write-read approach invented by our youngest son, Mike, before I began to teach. We could begin with Tilly Turtle.

Having three siblings and two parents who read to him frequently, Mike noticed that we all said exactly the same words when we read his books. He suspected that those wriggly black marks under the pictures must direct us what to say. One morning just before his fourth birthday he climbed up beside me while I was trying to relax with the Sunday paper. Seeking attention, he pointed to a large letter, S, in the headline and asked, *What's that?* Trying to match my answer to his maturity level, I shared, *It looks a bit like a snake, doesn't it? Sometimes snakes talk to each other like this, S S S S S.* Mike slipped to the floor, wriggling around, *I'm a snake, S S S S S.*

Later, when I was doing the breakfast dishes, he dragged a sheet of the paper into the kitchen and pointed to a letter, S, in the fine print. *This one is only a worm. What does a worm say?* I told him that worm's voices are so quiet that we can't hear them.

That same evening Mike announced at the dinner table, *Now I know your secret. I know why letters talk like that snake in the newspaper. It's because they're really noisy animals, but you can only see their skeletons. You call their skeletons, letters. When you read you look at the skeletons and make the animal noises.*

We didn't understand what he was trying to tell us. So to demonstrate his theory he went to his chalkboard and made a primitive lower case, *r. This one looks like a stick with a rainbow on top. What noise does that one make?* Jerry supplied a long growl, *r r r r r.* Mike stared for some time at his letter and repeated his brother's sound. Then he began to add a few more drawing strokes to his letter, crudely drawing a rooster with the letter as a scaffold. Above his drawing he drew a circle and wrote more *r* letters inside. *That's the talking balloon.* He grinned proudly over his production. *See! My rooster says, r r r r r. That's how you know what to say when you read. You just make the animal noises.*

Mike's Noisy Rooster

Living on our poultry ranch, Mike knew that roosters don't crow like COCK A DOODLE DOO in nursery rhymes. He had imitated rooster's crowing usually with five, R sounds in a row many times. He simply recorded what he knew to be true. I assured him that he was on the right track.

Perhaps the idea that marks on paper could represent noises might have been initiated in Mike's mind by his early interest in making music. Jerry had shown him how to pick out simple melodies on the piano by reading the notes. For several months Mike continued to play his letter game with us. He would select a letter from print, copy it on his chalkboard or a piece of paper and ask someone nearby what noise it represented. Then, repeating the noise, he would add a few strokes to the letter and crudely turn it into an animal with the *talking balloon* above.

Mike knew the conventional names for alphabet letters, but he never used them in his games. Instead, he made up stories about why each of his letter-animals made its specific noise. His letter, U, which he called a big smile, was the scaffold for a drawing of a baby duck who had been stepped on by a larger animal when it was just hatching. Instead of quacking, Mike's out of breath duck could only gasp, Uh Uh Uh. His letter, T, turned into a turtle that had misplaced her watch. She could hear it ticking, *T T T*, but she couldn't find it. For Mike's punch line the turtle finally remembered that her watch was hanging around her neck. She had put it there to keep dry while she was wading in her pond. At no time did Mike point out that this letter or its speech sound was the beginning for the word, *turtle.*

Perhaps he used animal noises because he was not much removed from that toddler stage when parents read animal stories and ask children to repeat their noises. *What does the cow say? MOOOO.* At any rate, his system worked for him. Eventually he began to write the letters without their cartooned animals and joined them into words. Then, somehow, he surprised us all by spontaneously exploding into self-taught reading before he was five.

Using our captive turtle, Tilly, to experiment with the Wooden Valley first graders, I told Mike's turtle story to them. I brought a noisy old alarm clock to school and we practiced making the ticking sound. The children wrote a T letter on their chalkboards. Then I showed them how to turn the letter into a turtle design like Mike did by making a circle around it and adding a head and four feet. We added a talking balloon with letters inside.

Johnny offered, *My turtle looks like it has a tattoo on its shell. My dad has a tattoo on his arm.* Then he insisted that we put a letter, T, on Tilly's shell in our aquarium. We satisfied him by using a felt pen and Tilly didn't seem to mind. I gave each of the four students a piece of our scarce paper and they spent the next hour happily drawing turtles, inventing scenarios, and sharing them with each other. I mounted their drawings on a bulletin board which I labeled, LETTERS AND SOUNDS. At recess time Johnny led the other three youngsters crawling around the playground and making ticking noises.

One letter down, twenty-five to go. Which letter should I try next? Again Johnny answered my question. He found a measuring worm crawling with its funny up and down walk down by the creek. We saved it in a glass until Gilman walked home at noon and borrowed a pickle jar to house our worm. He also brought some lengths of wood to keep our pickle jar from rolling off the table. Our nature study center was getting more interesting.

Lil found a picture of our new specimen in our encyclopedia and read to the class: *Sometimes it's called an inchworm because it's usually about an inch long. However, it's really a caterpillar that will metamorphose into a moth.* Gilman interrupted his brother, *Metamorphose means change.* Frankie noticed, *He's got some little tiny legs on the front and some on the back. Worms don't have legs, so the book is right. He has to be a caterpillar.* They named it, *Inchy.*

Gilman loudly shared his discovery in one of our nature books that in some parts of the world people eat worms. Of course the whole class responded loudly, *ihhhhhhhhhhhh!* This teaching opportunity was too valuable to ignore. All the students were at least six years old. Perhaps they were language mature enough to understand the alliteration principle by extracting the beginning sound of words. I pointed out that the noise they had just made was the first sound of Inchy's name. We used Inchy for our next letter and sound picture. We wrote a letter, *i*, on paper and drew worm skin around it with the talking balloon above and added these to our LETTERS AND SOUNDS bulletin board. At Benny's suggestion, we moved our science table with Tilly in her terrarium and Inchy in his pickle jar next to it under the drawings of the letter-animals.

When the third graders were working on a math unit on measurement they carefully let Inchy crawl up and down a ruler to further emphasize the quantity of one inch. Fascinated with his up and down crawl, this group began to imitate it. They placed hands and feet on the floor, walked hands out until their bodies were flat, then walked their feet up to their hands, back in Inchy's hump position. We had to take time out so all the children could practice this funny locomotion. At recess time, instead of baseball, we divided into four teams with mixed sizes and had an inch-worm relay race.

Lilburn Clark, Senior, the president of the school board, was driving by the school. Curious about our relay he stopped his truck and came to the playground to watch. Quietly he said to me, *It looks like you're turning them around. They're beginning to like going to school.* I thanked him and thought, *And I'm beginning to like being their teacher.*

Every day I read aloud from my own extensive library of alphabet books. The first graders were beginning to understand the format for the beginning sound of words. Even the migrant children could work with us because most Spanish speech sounds associated with consonant letters are the same as for English. The migrants did not need to understand the meaning of the words to play this learning game.

Johnny, our naturalist, then caught a ladybug. She escaped, flew around the room, then lit on Inchy's pickle jar. The four first graders wrote the letter, *l*, then used it for a scaffold for drawing a ladybug around it. They had learned three letters and their most common sounds in English. That was enough for our first sentence, *it lit.* All four beginners had learned the concepts of a letter, a word, and a sentence. We were on our way. Maybe I could really earn that credential. The children were consid-ering placing the ladybug in Inchy's pickle jar, but Lil insisted that we let her go outside. He explained that this was one of the good bugs that eat the bad bugs and help to save the crops.

The last week of our first month of school a curriculum supervisor from the county schools office spent the afternoon with us. When the students had all gone home she said that she approved of everything I had accomplished except my first grade reading program. Pointing to the chil-dren's drawing of Tilly and Inchy and the ladybug she shook her head from side to side. *You are trying to teach them phonics. It's impossible to pronounce a consonant sound in isolation as you are trying to teach them to do.*

Thinking about her statement, I remembered Willy, the Jones child in third grade who stuttered, *NNNNNNNO* when some child teased him. Sometimes when they thought he couldn't hear them the other children imitated Willy, *CCCCCan I hhhhhave a ttturn?* They didn't seem to have a problem pronouncing consonant sounds in isolation. But I didn't point this out to the consultant. She continued, *Phonics will slow down their progress in reading. Just have them memorize the words in their readers. It tells you how to do it in the teacher's manual for the books.*

I protested, *But what about Johnny? He won't even look at a book.* She was not concerned. *Just let him play. He's just not ready to read. Maybe he'll be ready next year. If he likes to draw, just let him draw about the characters in the books, Dick and Jane, Sally, Spot and Puff.*

Changing the subject, I showed her a stack of practice materials I had found in a cupboard at the rear of the room. Seeing her immediate frown, I knew she wouldn't approve. These folding cards had been designed with a single spelling pattern on each card so that by changing the beginning letter they could form new words. I had let the older students use them on Friday afternoons to practice their spelling. They liked to make up rhymes like,

The nurse
Will curse,
She lost her purse.

Mitchell, the sixth grader who scored about third grade reading level on my informal check, chose to use these patterned cards more than any other student. He lived with his grandparents because his mother was in jail and his father was in a mental institution. Dictating words to Mitchell from his sixth grade speller resulted in interesting, bizarre combinations of the words he knew how to spell, such as *younighted* for *united*. He had thoroughly memorized the words for spelling of numerals and used them regularly in his original sentences for spelling practice. *I went two the store four bread.* When I suggested to Mitchell that he try the fifth grade spelling book instead of the sixth his answer was traumatic, *NO! I DONE IT LAST YEAR! MY GRANDMA WILL HELP ME!*

The supervisor picked up the spelling pattern cards, then tossed them down on the table. *THESE ARE A WASTE OF TIME! Every English word must be memorized separately. There are too many exceptions to these patterns. Put these in your storeroom, or better yet, BURN THEM!* The spelling pattern cards went on a top shelf in Fort Knox. After all, she was the professional educator with experience. I didn't even have a credential.

There were six different levels of social studies materials in the storeroom, one for each grade. No way would it be feasible to do even a cursory coverage of all of them, so what topic would be suitable for the whole school to do together? With the presence of the migrant children it seemed pertinent to me to begin with a study of Mexico.

The older students, both resident and migrant enlarged a map of Mexico, which we hung on the wall nearest to the migrants' work area. We put the name of each of the temporary students on a paper flag attached to a colored map pin. Then, with Marta's help, we placed each pin at the home place for each of our migrants.

My Spanish dictionary helped me to explain to them, *Dibuja tu familia* (Draw your family). We mounted their family pictures around the map with colored strings attached to their place of origin. The resident students decided to duplicate the project for their own area when Lil brought a map of Wooden Valley donated by his father. They enlarged the map, then put a flagged pin in it for each child at the corresponding place of residence in the valley. Then they surrounded their map with their family pictures which they had drawn on the first day of school.

Of course we had to make a piñata. We inflated a large balloon. The students were then assigned in pairs, one resident and one migrant, to work on the task. They covered the balloon with strips of old newspapers soaked in wallpaper paste. We hung it to dry for a week, then deflated the balloon inside. Surprisingly it kept its shape. Finally the migrants painted the piñata in the colors of their Mexican flag—red, white and green. Pulling out the balloon left a hole at the top big enough to fill it with red, white and green jellybeans.

A discussion of Mexican foods led to an invitation to our migrant students to stay for lunch one day. Again, with the help of my dictionary, I composed a written invitation: *Puedes venir a la comida por favor, el miercoles a las 12 en punta.* (Please comes to lunch on Wednesday at 12:00.) The older students copied my Spanish on notepaper which I supplied, then the younger children decorated the invitations with red and green crayons.

The mother of our Martinez students helped us with the menu and the shopping list. Then, on party day, she supervised the making of tacos and refried beans. After lunch we tied the piñata to the branch of a tree and took turns taking a whack at it with our baseball bat. Finally Marta took a mighty swat and our piñata exploded with a hail of jellybeans for all. Lilburn Clark came to our party. He again mentioned to me that it looked like the children were liking school more and more.

Following the edict from the county curriculum supervisor I stopped using Mike's program showing the children how to turn alphabet letters into noisy animals. She might somehow interfere with my acquiring the credential promised by the superintendent. But it was too late. Watching the first graders, all the students in the school had learned to play the amusing letter and sound game. Even the migrants were writing letters and drawing animals around them, though most of them did not understand the concept. There was plenty of wild life around the school for letter-animal ideas. The students kept it up for months.

When I arrived at school one morning an unmistakable odor of skunk hung in the air. Following their noses, Frankie and Johnny found the source of the smell by the creek at morning recess. A mother skunk lay dead by the water. Her mangled body suggested that she had been hit by a car in the night and had crawled near the creek to die. Two uninjured kits were by her body. We found an empty carton in Fort Knox. Then Gilman and Lil caught the babies and placed them in the box. Gilman, our reference expert, shared with us, *I know the babies won't spray. They're too young. I read about it in a library book. It's the mother who made that smell.*

Lil went home for a shovel and we buried the mother in a deep hole by the creek. Benny insisted that we have a proper burial ceremony. *My grandma died and they played music.* So we sang our morning opening song, *My Country, 'Tis of Thee,* and closed with *Twinkle, Twinkle Little Star* and the *ABC* song. Back in school I phoned the State Fish and Game Department for help. The officer who took the orphan kits assured the children that they would be raised in an animal shelter until they could be released in the wild.

This incident inspired the older students to show the others how to draw skunks with their fuzzy black and white tails curled into an *S* shape. They put the talking balloons in the rear of the skunk drawing with more *S* letters inside to indicate the hissing sound of the spray.

The Clark's dog, Harry, came to school one afternoon, panting from the warm weather. The children gave him a drink and we let him stay. Shirley, watching him, giggled, *He's a smart dog. He can say the first sound of his name, Harry.* Beginning with the letter, *H* as a scaffold, cartoons of Harry appeared on the edges of worksheets. The hump of the lower case, *h*, was his back and legs with his tail up high. They added Harry's head on the side of the letter with his tongue hanging out. Each child's picture had a balloon above with *h* letters inside to indicate the panting sound.

Gilman made a home run during a post lunch baseball game. The ball landed in some brush at the edge of the playground. Katy, the fielder, chased the ball in the brush and her scream raised the hair on the back of my neck. OH, NO, A RATTLESNAKE zipped through my brain. Instead, a huge jackrabbit ran across the playground in big leaps, then disappeared in the vineyard. I laughed with relief and the children joined me. Back in the classroom it was time for our social studies. It was plain to see when I checked their papers that they were more interested in cartooning leaping jackrabbits beginning their drawings with the letter, *J.* Oh, well, the school board had told me that my major job was to help the children to like going to school. Johnny began to write his name beginning with his jackrabbit cartoon.

One morning Johnny was showing his jackrabbit cartoon to Juanito and trying to demonstrate the beginning sound of his name by pumping his bent arms as if he were jogging, but it was obvious that Juanito did not understand. Gilman, noticing the confusion, sat down with the boys to try to explain that the letter, *J,* represents a different sound in Spanish from English. First he cartooned another jackrabbit in front of Juanito's name. Then he pretended he was panting from running a long time.

A big smile of recognition spread over Juanito's face when he understood that his Spanish name begins with an exhale of breath. Then Gilman brought Jose, another migrant child, into their language game. The three little boys spent the next recess running around the school building and panting like fast jackrabbits. It was pleasing to see that Gilman had another side to his personality. He didn't always need to tease and be the center of attention. The mix of ages in our classroom gave such regular opportunities for children to develop compassion and respect for others.

Instead of noon baseball every day I suggested that we have more relay races some of the time. Again the students divided themselves fairly in equal-sized teams with Lil as the captain of one team and Mitchell the other. They alternated a large child and a smaller one in each line so the older ones could help the younger ones play. Johnny ran so fast that his team nicknamed him, *Jackrabbit Johnny.* The name stuck, but was shortened to, *Jack,* and Johnny asked me to show him how to write this new name.

The three first graders, Shirley, Katy and Frankie, were reading their preprimers about Dick and Jane one morning. It had been several weeks since Johnny had asserted his independence with a loud,

I'M NOT GOING TO LEARN TO READ,
AND YOU CAN'T MAKE ME DO IT !

I noticed that Johnny had lifted the lid of his desk and propped it open with a book, but I could not see what he was doing. Frankie, nearest to Johnny, silently mouthed to me, *He's reading with us.* I stood up so I could see inside Johnny's desk. His book was open to the same page we were reading and his finger was under the words. Obviously he was silently following our reading aloud. I put my hand on Johnny's shoulder. *Would you like to read with us?* Johnny slammed his desk shut, yelled, *NO! I CAN'T READ!* And ran out the door. By the time I reached the door he was on the road heading in the direction of home. I yelled, *QUICK! GILMAN ! GET HIM!*

All the class ran out to watch the drama, cheering Gilman chasing Johnny down the road while I silently prayed that any car coming around the bend in the road would see the runners. Jackrabbit Johnny was fast, but Gilman's longer legs won the race. He carried him piggyback back to school with Johnny beating him with his small fists.

Dismissing the class to the playground, I led Johnny into the classroom for a private conference. First I reminded him what had happened to the mother skunk and he promised he would not run out in the road again. Then I insisted, *You need to tell me now why you don't want to learn to read.* Johnny started to cry and I held him on my lap until it was over. Then it all poured out.

My mom said that if I don't learn to read I'll grow up
like my dad. He can't read. I want to be a truck driver
just like my dad. So I can't learn to read either.

I assured him that he could stay in school with us and draw his letter-animals. He wouldn't have to learn to read. I called the other students back into the classroom, but we didn't get much done the rest of the day. When I read to them during the last hour Johnny fell asleep and Lil carried him to the bus.

Certainly a conference with Johnny's parents was next, but how could I diplomatically approach this problem? His mother answered the telephone. I assured her, *No, Johnny is not in any trouble,* but we needed to talk. Next morning Johnny announced that he was not riding home on the bus. Instead his dad would pick him up in his truck after school. All day I worried, Would Johnny's father come in for our conference? Would he be defensive? Belligerent? Was he huge, like in Johnny's family drawing?

The other children went home on the bus. Johnny asked if he could draw on the big chalkboard while he waited for his father. Trying to correct papers, I couldn't concentrate. Did Johnny's family know that I had no teaching credential and this was my first real teaching experience? Johnny filled the wall with his letter-animal drawings and quietly sang the alphabet song to himself as he drew. It was almost four o'clock when a truck pulled into our driveway with two little boys in back—Johnny's look-alike stair-step siblings.

Johnny's father came in. Not what I expected, he was short and wiry, like Johnny. We sat at one of the large tables in the back of the room while I wondered how to begin. What should I say? I showed some drawings from Johnny's work folder. The father looked at the name in the corner, shook his head from side to side, frowned, and seemed to stiffen. *I don't want him called, Jack. His name is John.*

I called Johnny over to our table. *Would you tell your dad why you wrote, Jack, on your papers instead of your name, John?* Johnny smiled, *The kids call me, Jack, because I can run like a jackrabbit. I'm one of the fastest runners in the whole school.* The father relaxed, *He's like me. I was in track in high school. I dropped out in tenth grade. It seemed like a waste of time. I wasn't learning anything because I never learned to read.*

Johnny interrupted and looked at me. *See! I told you so. I'm not going to learn either!* Then he turned to his father. *I'm going to be a truck driver just like you when I grow up. I don't have to learn to read at school. I can draw all the time. See my letter-animals?*

He led his father to the chalkboard, showed him each letter and told him the story about each animal and the sound it made. I watched the demonstration for about ten minutes. The father seemed to be completely absorbed in Johnny's explanation, asking about each separate letter-animal. Then he turned to me. *Is that what they call phonics?*

I offered, *Some people might call it phonics. I just use this easy way to help beginners become aware of their own speech sounds that they use when they talk and the alphabet letters that represent those sounds for writing and reading.*

He added, *I never learned that. I only learned the names for letters, like A B C. I think that's why I never learned to read.* Johnny reached out for his father's hand. *If I learn to read, can I still drive a truck like you when I grow up?* His father reached out and hugged him. *Sure you can! You can run the whole truck business if you learn to read. You can be the boss!* Johnny pointed to his letter-animals on the chalkboard. *I'll show you how to make these and then you can be the boss too.*

The two little boys waiting in the back of the truck were getting impatient. Our conference came to a quick end. Too emotionally exhausted to correct any more papers, I locked the door and drove home over the mountain.

We celebrated all the holidays. The county agricultural extension division gave us some seedling trees. We planted them for Arbor Day near our lunch tables for future shade and sang Joyce Kilmer's, *Trees.* For Halloween we decorated gallon-sized ice cream cartons for loot buckets. But no ordinary citified trick or treat activities for these rural children. Instead they filled their buckets with over-ripe tomatoes from the fields and threw them at passing cars while hiding in the creek bed. The next morning at school there were tales of an unsuccessful attempt to push the old school building into the creek and of flying someone's underwear from the flagpole.

The migrants left as quietly as they came. We didn't even have a chance to say goodbye. One morning they didn't come and that was the end of them. By that time most of the children, both resident and migrant, were minimally bilingual.

By November the whole valley was red and gold with Fall color. Deer would sometimes pace my station wagon on the mountain road. When our calendar showed Veteran's Day I assumed that some of the students knew the purpose of this national holiday. When I asked if anyone could tell me the purpose of this special day Frankie volunteered, *The veterinarians are going to have a parade over in Fairfield.* Assuming that these rural children had experience with veterinarians, I asked, *What is a veterinarian?* Shirley spouted out, *I know! They don't eat meat!* Eventually we managed to get the definitions straightened out. Most of the students had relatives or close friends who had served in one of the wars of the century. We wrote thank you letters to them, made some flags, then had our own parade around the playground.

Writing the thank-you letters had been such a painful task for the students that I wondered what had turned them so violently opposed to independent writing other than filling in the blanks in workbooks. I had tried to get the older children to write a simple book report. David, the oldest of the Jones children leaned over my desk when I started to read his report. *DON'T YOU PUT ANY OF THOSE GODDAM RED MARKS ON MY PAPER!* Then it all became very clear. Their former teachers had obviously been so concerned with the mechanics of written composition, such as spelling, grammar and handwriting, that the students' messages seemed less important.

I had no guidance for teaching composition, but on reflection I realized that I certainly would not ever put any correction marks on a child's drawing. Would not putting correction marks on a child's written composition show the same disrespect?

I put my correcting pens and pencils in a bottom drawer in my desk so I would not be tempted to use them again. Then I asked the students to read their compositions to each other before they showed them to me. It was amazing to see how many simple errors they found when they turned their written language into spoken language. Reflecting on the difference between silent reading to one's self and reading aloud to another I realized these are different processes. When reading aloud we tend to read slower so errors in spelling and grammar are more obvious. Proofreading, I discovered, is better taught aloud and practiced in small groups. And corrections by one's peers are less threatening than corrections by a teacher.

With the pressure off for correct spelling in first drafts of original composition I decided to experiment with journal writing. I remembered seeing a stack of partially used old composition books in Fort Knox. Cutting out the used pages, I gave a book to each child. At first the students insisted that I assign a writing topic. Gradually they discovered that when they wrote about personal events their writing flowed more easily. They wrote longer and more interesting compositions with their own choice of topic.

Gilman, who usually found it so difficult to be quiet, burst out one morning, *Writing is just talking on paper!* Journal writing had given him a new outlet for verbal expression. He wrote several pages in his journal every day. It must have been therapy, because he was less noisy in the classroom. When Mitchell kept asking me to spell words for him, I responded, *Spell with your ears. Say the word you need aloud and slowly to yourself, listening to all the sounds you say. Then write what you hear.* Mitchell frowned. *But what if I spell it wrong?* I showed him that the red correcting pens and pencils were in the bottom drawer of my desk. Johnny intervened. *You can reach them if you stretch.* I opened my desk drawer, picked up all the red pens and pencils, put them in a shoebox, and placed the box on the highest shelf in Fort Knox.

At first the four youngest students only drew pictures in their journals. After several weeks they began to label parts of their drawings. They were spelling by ear: *sun, ski* for *sky, gras, apl tre, me, mi mom.* In their preprimers they had learned to read common words which do not follow standard English spelling patterns. We called them OUTLAW words. I made signs for these words with a string so they could be worn around the neck.

We chose one child a day to be the outlaw and wear
the word which did not follow a standard spelling pattern.

Gradually these four began to write *the, to, said, saw, was,* and short phrases using the conventional spelling of these words. To verify the spellings sometimes they checked in their readers. I began to realize that spelling by ear, which they did first, seemed to be a first step in spelling English.

Johnny always drew a picture before he wrote any words. The other three usually tried to write first, then illustrate their writing. Frankie asked Johnny why he drew the picture first and the logical answer was, *That's so I can remember what I'm writing about. If I forget, I just look at my picture.* Frankie followed Johnny's system and the girls soon followed. Their writing became more fluent. Johnny was the first one to write a whole sentence, and finally a short paragraph. The first grade reading also seemed to be more fluent. Johnny caught up with the others in spite of his independence and slow start.

One of the school board members, the Brown children's mother, visited one afternoon. She was an accomplished artist. Noticing some of the children's primitive drawings of faces, which I had posted on one wall, she volunteered to help them improve their drawings. She used her own Shirley for a model and pointed out that our eyes are on the same level as our ears, not up in the forehead like some of them had drawn. All the children enjoyed this face-drawing lesson so much that she agreed to come again.

Mrs. Brown told me that our school was expected to have a Christmas program for the whole Wooden Valley community. Traditionally it had been a play performed at the Farm Center, which had a stage. After weeks of worry, I asked the older children who had done this for several years what we should do. The consensus indicated that former plays had been dull and we should write our own. This seemed to me to be too much of an undertaking, but the students insisted.

Leading a discussion with the whole class, I told them that we needed to invent a problem related to the holiday, develop a plot, and come to a climax with a happy ending. The problem they decided on was that one of Santa's elves was such a klutz with tools that his toys didn't turn out right. The solution was to send him into the kitchen to help Mrs. Claus. The students' interest in alphabet letters developed the plot. The clumsy elf learned to read by putting things away by their beginning letters. The crisis occurred when Santa's glasses were accidentally broken on Christmas Eve.

He couldn't read the tags to deliver the gifts. The elf was pressed into service to ride with Santa. Gifts were delivered and the elf that could read the tags was hailed as a hero. We wrote the play together in our afternoons. Its rhyming format was natural for these young children, beginning,

This is the story of Elmer, the elf,
Who lived at the North Pole with Santa, himself.

The students voted to have Gilman with the loudest voice read their poem. The action would all be in mime. That way we had enough parts for everyone. Johnny, the smallest, was unanimously selected to be the clumsy elf. Lil and the oldest Martinez girl played the parts of Santa and Mrs. Claus. The rest of the smaller children were elves and the large ones were reindeer. They made pointed elf hats and cardboard reindeer antlers for their costumes.

The farm center was packed the night of our performance. All the ranch families in the valley attended. My husband, John, and our four children also came. At the end of our performance, Big Tony, who ran the only store in the valley, Ho Ho Hoed in a Santa costume at the door and brought candy canes for all the children. Several parents commented to me that their children complained less about going to school than in former years. No one said, however, that his or her children seemed to be learning anything.

The Fall semester was almost over and so far I had survived. The holidays came and went. My own four children seemed to be thriving in spite of my full-time job so far away from home. Cindy had a man teacher who seemed to be giving her individual attention, which she needed to catch up with her peers. She had been so wriggly in the primary grades that it had been difficult for her to pay attention. She was on a swim team now which used up some of her excess energy. Because Mike was such a strong reader the principal of his school recommended that he be transferred into first grade instead of kindergarten, but he refused to make the change. The highlight of his school day was riding the kindergarten bus and he would miss that if he were moved into first grade. His school compromised by giving him permission to read with the first grade when he chose to do so.

I had another week of vacation to reflect on the past months and to plan for any changes in routine at school. Except for Mitchell, all the students seemed to be gradually improving in their reading and writing skills. Although Johnny still had an occasional outburst, none of the children protested having to attend school. Perhaps I was achieving the school board's main assignment, to make school an enjoyable place to be. I could not, however, just plan for fun and games. Morally, I still felt obligated to show the students that learning to learn was exciting and pleasurable.

I realized that I had been giving minimal attention to math, but perhaps this had been subconscious. In my own father's Navy career we had moved frequently as he was transferred from base to base. I attended five different schools before my sixth grade and each school had different expectations. With each move I was either ahead or behind my classmates. The school I attended for second grade decided my reading level was too advanced for that grade, so they skipped me to the third grade. No one bothered to fill in my second grade gap in math. The result was that I went from simple counting and adding in first grade to multiplication in third. Ever since that skipped year I had been insecure in any situation requiring subtraction, the concept usually stressed in second grade. I knew how to do it, even the borrowing and carrying, but I always double-checked my subtraction to be sure. Usually I banked by mail because bank tellers, so quick with their figuring, somehow always seemed to be aware of my insecurity. Perhaps, I fantasized, there was a sign like an invisible, S, tattooed on my forehead, which lights up when I enter a bank.

A new published math program had been adopted by the school board and I was the first Wooden Valley teacher to use it. Instead of a separate teacher manual for each grade level, this publisher had combined both the teacher's directions for lessons and a copy of the student book. Each page of the student book was duplicated in full size on the right side of each page of the manual. On the left side of the page were explicit directions for the teacher. This made the combined manual for each of the six grade levels about ten inches high, eighteen inches across, and one and one-half inches thick.

Every day after school I loaded my station wagon with six of these ponderous books. Then, in the evening, after all my children were tucked into bed, I reviewed all six math lessons for the next day. So far I had kept up with the students and could answer simple questions. During the Fall no unfamiliar concepts had been introduced in these books, so the students hadn't yet suspected my personal math insecurity.

Now it was time to introduce fractions and decimals to the older students. During the last week of the holiday I went over and over those pages in the fifth and sixth grade manuals, memorizing all the words on the left side of each page. The first day back at school in January I was thoroughly prepared to teach a lesson on multiplying fractions, so I gathered all the fifth and sixth graders on the floor near the side-wall chalkboard.

Following the directions in the manual I wrote a demonstration problem on the board explaining each step as I proceeded. Briefly turning my back to the group, I picked up an aged wooden pointer from the chalk tray to review the steps in the problem with the group. Out of the corner of my eye I saw Gilman elbowing his neighbors on the floor. So, instead of using the pointer for my math lesson, my arm flew out and the pointer lightly tapped Gilman on the shoulder. Horrified, I watched the pointer break in two.

Gilman picked up the pieces and handed them back to me, and nobody said a word. Should I apologize? I had barely tapped him to get his attention. The ancient pointer must have been cracked. But I had used it as a weapon against the son of the president of the school board. There goes my credential! Too upset to think clearly about multiplying fractions, I dismissed the students back to their desks. Gilman volunteered that there was another pointer back in the storeroom. I thanked him, remembering it standing in a corner there, but I never used a pointer again. It is too easy to use it as a weapon. Abandoning group math lessons, I called individual students to my desk instead when they encountered a new concept. That way, with one-to-one encounters, my math insecurity was less obvious.

In mid-January the weather turned very cold so the road over the mountain was covered with ice in the early morning. The tallest peak, George, to the east, kept the sun from hitting the road to melt the ice until later in the day. Unfamiliar with icy roads, I panicked when my station wagon lost traction and slipped from side to side. There was no barrier to keep from going down over the cliff. I could not turn around, so the only thing I could do was keep climbing to the top and hoping I would not meet another car. The downgrade was the sunny side of the mountain, so all I had to do was to get to the top.

February was warmer, but this is California flood season. In town the Napa River flowed over its banks and the creeks flowed over my mountain road. Except for one morning when there was a mudslide at each end of the road, I managed to get to school on time. Whenever the rain stopped long enough to let the children outside to the playground they *accidentally* fell in the puddles. We lined up wet shoes in the entry and were grateful to the school's architect for radiant heating in the floors. One day a psychologist from the County Schools Office dropped by for a visit. Noticing the bare-footed students, he remarked, *They're so relaxed!* Everyone was relaxed except Teacher.

A notice came in the school mail about a university extension course being offered two evenings a week. It was to be held in Fairfield, about a half hour drive from Wooden Valley. The course, titled Remedial Reading, might show me how to help Mitchell. And some decision-maker would realize I was serious about acquiring a credential. My husband, John, agreed that he could prepare dinner for our children two nights a week for six weeks. On those days I worked all afternoon at school, correcting papers and workbooks until 6:00, went to the class from 7:00 to 9:00 and did not get home until 10:00. Then I had to go over the ponderous teacher manuals for math to prepare lessons for the next day.

Mitchell had begun to live with his grandparents in his fifth grade, so he had only been at Wooden Valley for one year. Apparently he had not had the same strong instruction as Lil and Gilman in his early school years. The college instructor told me that Mitchell was typical of students who were first taught with what she called *sight-reading*. Because he did not understand the alphabetic phonetic system of English, she said he was probably a victim of *memory overload*. Typically, she explained, it becomes evident between second and third grade. Then reading progress slows down year by year. She suggested that I try to show Mitchell common word patterns so he would not have to remember every separate word. I remembered the spelling cards with word patterns that I had found back in September. Mitchell had used them more than any other student. Back then, at the insistence of the county curriculum supervisor, I had hidden them away on a top shelf in Fort Knox.

I retrieved the cards and hid them in a bottom drawer in my desk. Mitchell and I practiced with them when the other students were busy with their reading workbooks. I hoped the supervisor wouldn't surprise us with an unannounced visit. One day I praised Mitchell for his progress with the patterned cards and he confided, *My grandparents who take care of me are getting very old. I can't live with them for many more years. I need to learn to read well enough so I can pass the test to get into the Navy. My grandpa says the Navy will take care of me forever.*

I still read to the students every afternoon. Sometimes it was a chapter from the classics, like Robinson Crusoe. Sometimes it was an old favorite for the younger children. Since the success of our Christmas drama, occasionally the children would decide to replay the story. They did Cinderella over and over again, making up their script as they went along. The boys took turns being the handsome prince, even Lil and Mitchell. The first time I read Billy Goats Gruff perhaps I was too dramatic with the trolls threatening the little goats. I noticed a very serious face on Johnny's face and his worried expression. I stopped and asked, *Is this a really real story or just pretend?* All the children agreed that it was just pretend, except Johnny.

He protested loudly, *NO! My dad tells me about those mean old trolls who hide under bridges. They come out and catch you. My dad calls them the highway trolls.* In the western states the State police system is called the Highway Patrol. No doubt Johnny's dad, with his job as truck driver was voicing his experience with the *highway trolls.*

The two Brown children came down with chicken pox, but it didn't spread to the other students. Apparently the Wooden Valley children had already had it earlier. Unfortunately, Mrs. Brown was not immune because she picked it up from her children. Major complications developed and she did not survive. The students had so enjoyed her drawing lessons, so of course they were devastated. When the Brown children returned to school their father stayed with them for a full week before he had to return to his ranch duties. In addition to helping all of us through an emotional time, he was an invaluable math aide, particularly for the older students.

In March the mushrooms magically popped up everywhere. One morning when I reached the top of the mountain all three children from the Jones family were waiting beside the road for the school bus. They lived on an isolated ranch a mile from the road. Stopping my station wagon, I piled the children onto the rear seat. They were unusually quiet. Finally David, the oldest, offered, *We almost lost Ma last night.* I did not want to pry, but the serious faces in my rear view mirror suggested more, especially after our grief in the loss of Mrs. Brown. The others all began to talk at once, then David took the lead. *You know Big Tony down at the store? He knows all about the wild mushrooms. He knows which ones are the good ones and which ones are the bad ones. WELL, HE DON'T!*

Then David continued, *Big Tony brought Ma some of his wild mushrooms yesterday morning. She cooked some and ate them for lunch. She got very sick and she was all alone. Dad was at work with the car and we were all at school. We don't have a phone, so Ma had to walk over to the Martinez house. It's almost a mile through the woods. Mrs. Martinez took her to the hospital. Ma is still very sick, but she didn't die.*

Parking my car beside the school, I unlocked the door to let the Jones children inside. Approaching my desk I noticed it was crawling with hundreds of tiny insects. Martin, the youngest Jones, was at our science table. He squealed, *COME, SEE! THEY'RE HATCHING!* In the Fall Johnny had found a praying mantis. We put the insect in the pickle jar with Inchy. That was a mistake! The mantis ate Inchy for lunch. It was a fascinating insect to watch. It also must have thought we were interesting too because it turned its head to watch us, like an owl, when we came close. Gilman, our reference specialist, found out from his reading that, because of its large size, our mantis must be a female.

I explained to the children that when writing about this insect, they could spell its name two ways. Sometimes it can be spelled PREYING MANTIS because it preys on other insects and eats them. For that reason, I told them, it is good to have one in your garden to eat the bad insects that eat your plants. Then I added that sometimes its name is spelled, PRAYING MANTIS, because it hold its front claws together to eat its food. It looks like it is praying. Shirley chuckled, *I know! It prays before it eats. We do that at home sometimes.*

We had placed a screen over the opening to the pickle jar. One morning I noticed a large tan mass on the under side of the screen. It looked like someone had squashed a graham cracker on it. Pointing to the jar, I asked, *WHO MADE THIS MESS?* There was a chorus of, *NOT ME*'s Gilman looked up from his book, *Oh, I know what that is. She must have laid some eggs.* He came over to the pickle jar and looked at the tan mass. *Yes, that looks just like it did in the book.* We couldn't keep the mantis supplied with enough insects to satisfy her voracious appetite, so one day we let her go. We kept the egg case on the screen, but I did not think they would really hatch. Obviously I was mistaken.

The babies looked just like their mother, only in miniature, each about one quarter of an inch long. There were hundreds of them all over the classroom. Like their mother, they were hungry and eating each other. When the rest of the students arrived we all took jars to catch as many of the babies as we could. We let them go outside so they could forage for themselves. It was noon before we stopped finding them.

As the spring weather warmed the earth the valley was suddenly covered with wild flowers, bright orange California poppies, purple lupine and yellow buttercups. The mountain sides were thick with Iris in shades of blue, purple, yellow and striped as well. We took a nature walk one day after lunch, gathered flowers, pressed them, and later turned them into wall plaques to save as gifts for Mothers' Day. This was the best art project of the year. It was also the best lesson in how to catch poison oak. We all itched and scratched for weeks.

Between the rows of grape vines the mustard plants grew tall. I looked down from the mountain every morning on a sea of gold. In the field next to our school the mustard plants grew taller than our first graders. At recess time I let the students go into the field where they organized a maze of pathways through it. I hoped the snakes were sleeping.

The mustard coordinated with our Social Studies unit on California missions. I told the children the legend about Father Junipero Serra and the mustard seeds. *There were no roads when Father Serra traveled north into California from Mexico. He showed the Indians how to make clay bricks and then how to build a mission with them. When each mission was finished he would travel one day north to begin another mission. As he traveled he sprinkled mustard seed he had brought from Spain on the ground. When he returned in the Spring the mustard had sprouted. He could find his way back by following the blooming mustard flowers. They called Father Serra's road between missions the Via de Oro, meaning the road of gold. Today the mustard has spread all over California. When it blooms every Spring we remember Father Serra and his missions.*

Benny, the quiet one, volunteered, *That's just like Hansel and Gretel. Remember when they sprinkled bread crumbs so they could find their way home? Then the birds ate the crumbs and Hansel and Gretel were lost.* Perhaps all my story reading was beginning to pay off. Benny was only a second grader. But his offering indicated that he was seeing relationships between literature themes.

The warmer weather did encourage the snakes to venture out of their hiding places. Almost daily on the road I saw a dead snake that had been crushed by a car. One day Gilman killed a rattlesnake on the playground with a baseball bat. Then, at my invitation, an officer from the State Fish and Game department came to talk to us about snakes. He brought a movie showing which snakes were dangerous and which ones should be left alone because they eat mice and other small rodents which destroy crops. He helped us skin the rattler that Gilman had killed. We used the skin for a lesson on measuring.

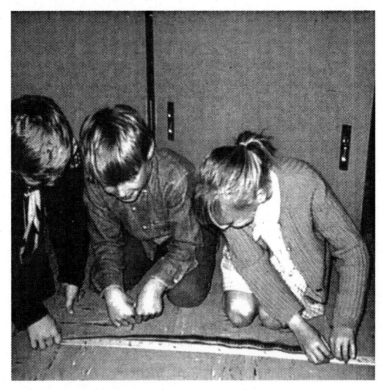

We used the rattlesnake skin
for a lesson on measuring.

This exciting event inspired all the students to draw and write snake stories. I had to spend so much time every evening planning for the next day's math lessons that I had little time to carefully review their snake compositions. It was apparent, though, that when they didn't need to be concerned with conventional spellings their writings became longer and more interesting. I explained that writing and spelling are different activities. The school board had ordered grade level spellers and we used them faithfully on Friday afternoons. Then I noticed that when there was no pressure to spell correctly in their free writings, their conventional spelling magically improved in assigned spelling projects. More and more I learned that learning to spell by ear is an important step in learning to spell correctly. Mitchell's spelling improved dramatically when he learned to listen to his own voice and record letters for the speech sounds he heard.

The extensive work on the road went on all school year. It was being widened to plan for heavy traffic to a new man-made lake in the valley just north of us. The new dam and lake would provide more needed water for the growing population, but would fill that valley and engulf the entire town of Monticello. One afternoon we all took a walking field trip through the vineyards to the new road.

We watched the workmen pushing dirt around
with their enormous machinery.

A foreman for the project sat with us and told us the names and task for each one—bulldozer, scraper, grader and compactor. Then, at my request, the manager of a local tractor company brought us some pictures of these machines and loaned us a set of miniature earth moving equipment. We all went outside where he demonstrated the use of each one in a pile of dirt. For days afterward the children used these toys to build their own road in one corner of the playground which had not been surfaced.

Because of the children's interest, the school board granted my request for a school bus so we could take a field trip to the site for the new dam and lake being constructed. We spent a whole day in Monticello, visiting their town hall, their farm center and their stores. We ate our lunch in the town square. Then, in the afternoon, we talked with students in their own one-room school like ours. These students' families would soon have to move before their town was under water. Some of the children belonged to families who had lived in their valley for several generations. One child told us his family had lived there for over a hundred years.

On the way home I asked the bus driver to stop at the top of the mountain. We all got out and looked down over the town of Monticello and the valley, which would be covered with water the following summer. The children had been noisy on the morning bus ride, but on the ride home it was not necessary to quiet anyone. The students and I were all thinking the same thoughts. Then Benny expressed it for us. *It's really sad for them, but I'm glad it's not our own Wooden Valley.*

Of course our trip led to several afternoon discussions concerning the environment and the need for conserving water in lakes to serve the state's fast growing population. *When I go fishing in the new lake next year,* commented Frankie, *I'm going to remember the Monticello school way down under the water.* Gilman laughed, *Maybe that's why they call it a school of fish.* He failed, however, to explain his word play to the younger children.

In April my triple role of parent, teacher and college student began to be too much. My body was showing signs of overload. On the evenings when I did not go to my Remedial Reading class I played my mother role, holding myself together until everyone was in bed. Then, when it was time to tackle the math books, I started to shake all over. When the shaking wouldn't stop the tears began to flow. So I gave up and went to bed. Our family doctor prescribed tranquilizers. Each week he changed my prescription to a different kind, but none of them worked.

Finally the college class was over. The shakes were still there, but not so aggravated. With my fatigue, I became less patient with the children. One afternoon Gilman was at his noisy worst. He had finished his own work and was bothering the rest of the students. Finally, I burst out, *GILMAN, GO HOME! We'll see you in the morning.* He picked up his lunch box and headed out the door toward his home one half mile down the road.

Within thirty minutes he was back at school driving a small tractor around and around the school building while all the students stood at the windows waving at him. It was not a good day.

In May the girls began to wear cotton dresses to school instead of jeans. Our school year was winding down. I bribed the children with gold stars to put on extra speed and finish all projects under way. I had read that the desire to learn should be sufficient motivation. But it was easier to work on the American spirit of competition. Friday afternoons we had award ceremonies. We used up all the boxes of stars in all colors, all the old Christmas seals, Easter seals and assorted stamps I could lay my hands on. Each award ceremony ended with a cookie treat for all.

The last week of school I was working at my big oak desk making out report cards. The last load of students had left. It was already June and, if possible, I was even more anxious than the boys and girls for summer vacation to come at last. The schoolroom was a complete shambles. Skipping clean up time, we had worked up to the last minute on a spelling exercise, which I had felt was more important at the time. Looking at the mess, I began to wonder. All was quiet except for a distant tractor in the prune orchard down the road and the buzzing of an enormous bee. It had entered uninvited through the open door and was demanding to be let out through the window behind my desk.

With mixed feelings of sympathy and self-preservation I stood up to open the window when an expensive looking car stopped in front. A handsome gentleman with black hair and shiny dark eyes quietly walked into the room. He was loaded with professional-looking photographic equipment. With the trace of an accent, he asked if he might take some pictures of our school—and of ME! This was the first one-room school he had encountered in his travels.

We dusted off our world globe and I posed for him pointing, at his request, to Iran. He glanced out our north window at the bright green hills with the grey-blue mountains beyond. With obvious nostalgia he shared, *Your valley reminds me of my own home.* Surprised, I insisted, *On this map Iran is all tan, like desert. I always think of that part of the world as sand dunes and oil wells.* Patiently he explained, *In the northern part of Iran where I live there are rolling green foothills. Much of it is covered with jungle growth. We raise cattle. At home I am a cowboy!* A cowboy from Iran! I conjured up the scene when I would explain to my husband and children why I was delayed after school.

My unusual guest continued to use rolls of film, all the time asking questions about our one-room school, which he seemed to think unique. *So expressive,* he suggested, *of the American desire for independence in thought and action regardless of the cost in dollars and cents.* He was so right. Rather than consolidate with an adjoining school twenty minutes away by school bus, the residents of Wooden Valley voted to build this new school for eighteen children for the staggering sum at that time of forty six thousand dollars. My visitor went out to the playground to take a few more pictures while I waited outside to say goodbye. Sensing my curiosity, his driver explained that I had been entertaining Prince Goodarz Khan Bakhtiari whose family had ruled the nomadic Bakhtiari tribe of Iran for the past five centuries. *He's a first cousin of Queen Soraya. She's also a Bakhtiari. The prince, here, acted as talent scout for the Shah. He sent pictures of Soraya when the Shah was looking for a queen.* I pictured myself as pin-up in some sultan's palace. American country schoolteacher, no less! The prince took pictures of me too!

When the prince returned to his car he thanked me for showing him the school. He asked about my family, so I told him about my husband, also a teacher, and our four school age children. Then he asked if he could visit our home in Napa *to see how an average American family lived,* so of course I invited him. The following day I went home directly after school and we entertained the prince in our patio in the back of the house. We served tea and the children were on their best behavior. It's not every day you get to entertain a real live prince.

Prince Goodarz Khan Bakhtiari

We had a graduation party for Lil, Mitchell and Tanya Martinez. I wrote a note in Mitchell's folder before I sent it on to the junior high in town recommending that he receive special help. Lilburn Clark came to our party and requested that I return to teach at Wooden Valley for a second year. He told me that I had fulfilled the school board's expectation. All the children now liked to go to school.

Then the county supervisor told me about a kindergarten opening near my home in Napa Valley—one session in the morning and another in the afternoon. This assignment would still serve for my second year to qualify for a teaching credential. It saddened me to think about leaving Wooden Valley, but our family physician strongly recommended that I find a less stressful job while I still had young children at home. At the end of my last day at Wooden Valley I drove up the mountain over the newly widened road. At the top a doe and her spotted fawn faced me, as if to say goodbye, then bolted into the pine forest.

As the county superintendent had told me, *The State Department of Education believes that experience on the job is more valuable than any Education Courses.* For the next 25 years of teaching, even after acquiring a number of credentials and degrees, I relied primarily on what I had learned that year at Wooden Valley.

After Wooden Valley

KINDERGARTEN

The principal who interviewed me for the job opening was unusually frank, *I'm very prejudiced against you. But you have had preschool experience and I'm desperate for a kindergarten teacher.* When I was signing my contract she did share her prejudice was caused by hearing, probably from the county supervisor who was assigned to me at Wooden Valley, that I had taught alphabet skills and phonics to my first graders instead of following the teacher's manual for the Dick and Jane reading program. In addition, there were rumors that I was primarily interested in teaching gifted children.

I didn't bother to remind the principal that my first experiences were with special children with an assortment of impairments who were anything but gifted, with the possible exception of deaf Tom and blind Jenny. And all the Wooden Valley students seemed to be just normal rural children. I wasn't even sure what a gifted child might be.

In spite of that interview the year went smoothly enough, and as my family physician suggested, it was easier. Kindergarten wasn't a whole lot different from my former experiences with my own children in preschools. I was especially careful to follow what I thought would be my principal's expectations. I did not want her to get in the way of my acquiring the promised credential at the end of my second teaching year. Some of the other teachers at my school quietly warned me that each year the principal selected one teacher to receive the brunt of her constant criticism and that this year it would probably be my turn.

During my original interview she had been so adamant against my teaching the speech sounds represented by alphabet letters as I had done at Wooden Valley. Consequently I avoided any introduction of alphabet skills. I did not even hang a traditional alphabet chart on the wall. The only visible words were two large labels, BOYS and GIRLS for the two classroom bathrooms. One afternoon after school the principal and another county curriculum supervisor came into my classroom. Without speaking to me the supervisor yanked down the sign for boys and the principal followed her with the sign for girls. When my mouth flew open with astonishment, the supervisor explained her actions, *Young children should not be exposed to printed words. It will cause them to be nearsighted.*

To distinguish the two bathrooms I then replaced the labels with a picture of a boy and another of a girl. The first child to notice the change the next morning asked, *Why can't we put signs there like the gas stations have? They say MEN and WOMEN.* Then he added, *The sign that says WOMEN has the word, MEN on the end of the word. My dad says that it looks like it says, WHOA MEN. I like to read signs.* Later, in our library corner, I noticed that he didn't hold the book near his face. Maybe he wasn't nearsighted yet.

The children began to mount their own drawings of boys and girls on the doors. They took special care to distinguish gender with special clothing and hair styles. Occasionally a picture would be correctly labeled, BOY, or sometimes BOYZ. GIRL or GIRLS usually appeared as GRIL or GRILZ. And nobody came in to tear down the children's own signs.

Two girls in my first kindergarten began to read books to each other. It was obvious that they had already figured out the English written language system. I asked their mothers how they had learned to read. Both parents were apologetic, indicating that they had not encouraged this practice, but that it had been completely self taught.

Susan was fascinated with the rhythm and visuals of television commercials. Her self-taught game of memorizing commercials gave her a basic written vocabulary, which she then applied to her storybooks. She had learned to read the word, COMET, by watching the commercial for this cleansing powder. She transferred it to the word, COME. I noticed that, even though she understood the meaning of COME, when she read it aloud she pronounced it like CALM, as in COMET, rather than her normal conversational pronunciation, CUM.

Maureen, according to her mother, was very eager to learn to read to compete with her first grade brother. At home she regularly took a beginning picture dictionary to her bed at afternoon rest time. One day she announced to her mother that she could read all the words in her dictionary. Her mother covered the picture clues and Maureen recited all the words. With this basic vocabulary she went on to read books. Neither of these girls showed any signs of being nearsighted yet.

One day at our library corner Peter pointed to the word, *thinking,* in a book and asked me what it said. When I supplied it for him he continued, *It looks like it says, king, on the end. What does the front part say?* When I supplied the word, *thin,* for him he delightedly discovered, *You can put little words together with no space between and they make big words!* As if to verify his discovery, Peter than took crayons and paper and drew a picture of a person with a crown on its head. Above his king there was a large balloon in the comic book format. In his balloon there was a smaller picture of a person wearing a dress and a picture of a baby. Under his picture Peter wrote, *This is a thin king thinking about getting maryd.*

Peter discovers that short words put together
make long words

Sam, another five-year-old, already was a fluent writer and was fascinated with our bizarre English spelling system. One morning he set out to find how many ways he could spell the word, *queen*. To systematically attack his problem, he first copied the word across the top of a large piece of paper at our painting easel. Then, under each of the letters he wrote all the other ways he knew how to represent the four speech sounds in his word, *queen*. Finally, by combining letters in various ways, Sam invented ten new ways to spell his word. I had read that in Shakespeare's time alternate spellings were considered the mark of a highly literate individual. Shakespeare frequently varied spellings, including his own name.

Sam invents ten ways to spell, queen

My former beginners at Wooden Valley did not seem so fascinated with the mechanics of written language. Could it be that those children were older, some six and some already seven, instead of just late fours and fives like my kindergarten students? I had read some research indicating that the ability to make fine discrimination of sounds comes to a peak between ages two and five and then tapers off.

This is certainly evident in the Japanese success with teaching music by ear to preschoolers. Perhaps that is why very young children can effortlessly speak two or more languages. Could it be that I was so concerned with starting my Wooden Valley beginners on reading that I had not first encouraged this writing play which I was observing in kindergarten? Should writing precede reading instruction?

I began to take more evening and summer college courses to try to find some answers. One of the most interesting reports was by Maria Montessori written in the beginning of the twentieth century. She was assigned to work with what they called, *defective* young children, in the slums of Rome. From her observations she determined, *Show young children how to write and then they will spontaneously explode into reading.* She also wrote, *Writing is easier than reading because children know what they have written. In reading they must interpret the thoughts of others, a much harder task.*

Also from my reading I found a survey of children who learned to read before instruction in school. The author indicated that all her early readers were also early *scribblers.* They went on long self-imposed binges of copying letters, words, numerals and even whole calendars. Following this lead, when a new principal was assigned to my school at mid-year, I gained permission to add a writing center to my kindergarten. There the children were encouraged to scribble and draw, copy letters and words, and make signs for various activities. I observed that the students who chose to use the writing center most often were the most active, noisy children, particularly boys. Could it be that Writing, a doing task, appealed to their hands-on, do-it-myself approach to learning?

Bret writes, it is fun to rit.

Chris writes, it Wuz Mi trn to Be uP in Cic Bol.

Marquis writes, *I lic 2 pla socr.*

Joel writes, *CAMRON CICT The BOL iN Mi I.*

It seemed like I was destined to teach children who were different from the average. The day before the next school year started I was getting the kindergarten room organized and decorated when a man and woman entered and introduced themselves as the parents of one of my new students. The mother said she wanted to give me fair warning about her Robert. He had been badly burned in an accident the previous year and the healing had stretched the skin on his face. Some timid children might interpret his appearance as scary like a Halloween mask. She mentioned that their neighbor children accepted Robert because they had known him before his accident.

I suggested that Robert not come to school until the second day, giving me time to prepare the rest of the children. The first morning I went through the ritual of showing new students how to raise a hand when I called out a name. Then I told them that another child would join us the following day. *He looks a little bit different because his face was burned in a fire.* When Robert arrived the next morning no child stared, and no one asked questions about his appearance. He was one of the gang from the beginning, a normal little boy whose face looked different.

In the summer my State teaching credential had arrived in the mail, just as the county officials had promised me. Now the superintendent couldn't tell me, *THAT IS ONLY YOUR LAY OPINION!* Perhaps now I would be allowed to have some professional opinions of my own.

The new principal seemed like he would be more reasonable. He saw no reason why I should not teach alphabet skills to kindergarten students. Now I could try the draw-write-read program that had worked so well with reluctant Johnny back in Wooden Valley. This time, though, there would be 30 students in the morning and another 30 in the afternoon instead of just four beginners. Would it work with such large groups?

Introducing reading instruction with the students' own names, I began to call the roll silently, holding up individual cards for recognition. The children seemed to enjoy this game and often commented on names with the same letters in them. Joe and Tom discovered simultaneously that each had a round O letter in the middle of their names. Matching of letters then became a self-imposed searching game for all students. Some children began to trace letters in the air that they saw on the roll cards. Capitalizing on this activity, I encouraged all students to do this magic invisible writing in the air. Often the traced letters would then appear as painting designs or borders on a drawing. At circle time on the rug when the children faced each other some students objected that the students across from them were *making letters backward.*

None of the books I had read on early literacy and none of the college courses I had begun to take mentioned the importance of students facing in the same direction during any letter practice. I changed our seating arrangement from the traditional circle time. Instead the children sat in several rows facing me instead of facing each other.

Many of these important clues were coming to me primarily by observation of students. Textbooks on Education often mentioned that beginners learn best in active hands-on ways. I wondered if any of us ever outgrow that way of learning. It seemed that what I had learned so far about teaching was by actual hands-on teaching, from personal experience and from making errors.

I left the roll cards in the writing center and before long most of the students could write their own names. Observing name writing it was obvious that this task was not equally difficult for all students. Names with diagonal lines in the letters seemed to be the hardest to make. One day I observed Mary trying to make her capital M. Trying to encourage her and pointing to the vertical line she had already made, I said, *Now stop and think. Where are you?* Mary cried out in frustration, *I know where I am. I don't know where I am going!*

Apparently I was not alone in my interest in students' learning to make alphabet letters. I found a study about the ages at which certain letter strokes can be made. The random diagonal *windshield wiper* stroke appears early in scribbling. But the ability to direct diagonal strokes in a specific direction develops much later. I learned that the difficulty in drawing the diagonal stroke is that it moves in two directions at once, either up or down and either left or right. It was recommended that involving children in board games, like checkers, in which they would move markers in specific diagonal directions, would help. So I added checkers to our classroom table games.

In the Spring I decided it was time to begin my draw-write-read study. I arranged tables so that all children were facing me instead of each other to avoid directional confusion. I gave a sheet of newsprint and a black crayon to each child. Mounting a large sheet of paper on a painting easel for demonstration I showed the students where I wanted them to write their names, in the upper right corner. That is the place where teachers had always expected me to place my name when I was in school.

While the students were working on their names I walked around the room to see which ones were following directions. To my dismay, over half of the children had completely reversed their names, starting at the right edge and even reversing their letters. None of them had reversed names before. What was wrong with my directions? Then it all became very clear. Young students need a specific beginning place, such as the paper's edge. When I told them to put their names on the right side, that is where they began to write, the right edge, thus reversing their names.

I confessed to the children that I had made a big mistake. Then I turned my demonstration paper over and told them to do the same with their papers. This time I changed directions, showing them how to begin their names in the upper left corner. No child reversed a name. Why hadn't the Education courses taught me this? Experience was certainly the best teacher of teachers.

I read that the average child can make the vertical-horizontal cross at four years, one month, so I began instruction with the letter, T. I told the students the same story about Tilly Turtle that I had used back in Wooden Valley. Then I led them through the steps of drawing the turtle, using the letter, T, as a scaffold. Every child was successful. Now I knew I could do this with thirty children at a time, not just with my four beginners at Wooden Valley.

Every kindergarten day was a learning experience for me. One afternoon Jimmy brought a book for our Share and Tell time. Holding it up he announced, *This is my PTA book.* Encouraging Jimmy to share more details and expand his oral language delivery, I asked, *Did you get your book at the PTA book sale?* Giving me a disgusted look, Jimmy pointed to the title of his book. *Can't you see? It says right here, EncycloPTA.* Sure enough, he was sharing a children's encyclopedia.

The responsibility for the safety of 30 five year olds in the morning and another 30 in the afternoon kept me on my feet. To move rapidly I wore tennis shoes as I had learned to do back in the special education classes. One morning I wore a dress in a pink and yellow print. I could not decide whether to wear my pink or my yellow tennis shoes, so I wore one of each. The students glanced at my shoes, whispered among themselves, but to my surprise, no one mentioned my different colored shoes to me. Apparently they assumed it was a big mistake and they did not want to embarrass me. I overheard one girl explaining compassionately, *Her closet was dark. She couldn't tell the colors. Let's not tell her.*

Population in our community was rapidly expanding. Two new schools in adjoining neighborhoods to take care of the overflow would not be completed until the following summer. The State did not yet require school districts to offer kindergarten, so our school board voted to eliminate kindergarten for the school year. That way there would be more space for older students. Our kindergarten room was converted into a sixth grade classroom.

Then our principal offered an alternative arrangement, which was accepted by the school board, using the large multi-purpose room for our kindergarten setting. Another teacher, Zelda, and I were selected to teach 60 children in the morning and another 60 in the afternoon in this space. To avoid defending this makeshift arrangement to parents we introduced the outsized kindergarten as a great new experiment in team teaching and announced it in the local newspaper.

Our approach did not convince one group of parents who staged a protest meeting led by a few administrators from other schools whose children had been assigned to our team kindergarten. At the meeting, Mr.Arnold, a principal from another school, stood up and described how he had deliberately avoided sending his daughter to preschool so her initial school experience would be a psychological coming-of-age event in her life. He added that this could not happen unless she could make an important attachment to one teacher, not two. In addition, he insisted that two teachers would have different rules and expectations, which would be confusing to a young child.

Looking back, I know that I should have let this man's protest die a natural death. Instead, to defend our position, I responded, *Mr.Arnold, does your daughter have two parents?* To which he assented. *Do you and Mrs. Arnold have the same rules and expectations for your daughter? Does having two parents cause your daughter to be confused?* Both embarrassed and enraged, his face became flushed and he sat down. I won the battle, but I lost the war. For the next twenty years, when ever our paths crossed, Mr.Arnold made every effort to degrade my professional credibility. He even attempted unsuccessfully one time to have my teaching credential rescinded.

The team kindergarten was not my creation. We teachers were simply doing the best we could under very difficult circumstances. To assure parents that their children would not get lost in the crowd Zelda and I worked intensively to quickly learn all 120 names of the children and associate them with 120 faces. After each session we studied them together. One of us would read a name while the other would describe the child's appearance. In three days of strenuous study we learned all 120 names and faces.

To be sure all children headed home in the right direction we color-coded their name tags red, yellow and blue. The students lined up at dismissal time at one of three color-coded doors to match their name tags. We aimed them toward their three neighborhoods and hoped they would follow through. We didn't lose a one.

Using the large multi-purpose room to advantage, we set up our equipment for two separate playhouses for dramatic play. Then, playing the roles of two families, the children visited each other, sometimes even exchanging cooperative child care. Sometimes the boys, playing fathers, would stay home to care for their children while the mothers went shopping in our play store. The students were replaying their own lives.

Seating 60 children in the traditional circle on the floor was out of the question. Instead we found a large rectangular rug for seating. We divided it with duct tape into six rows. Then, when the students sat down on the rug for roll call or any other reason to have them together, they sat in six rows of ten children. In a short time they learned how to count to ten to get the exact number of children in each row. At roll call time we showed the students how to fold down one finger for each child present in the last row. Any still upright fingers told them how many children were absent for the day. Soon the students were proficient in reporting which children were missing. They quickly learned all number combinations to ten, then to count to 60 by ones, fives and tens. The rug provided our first math curriculum.

There were no bathrooms in our multi-purpose room. We borrowed the U.S. Navy term for a toilet as a HEAD. The HEAD teacher for the week then led red, yellow or blue groups in turn to bathroom facilities in another part of the school campus. We teachers, however, did not get a mid-session break.

Clearing a five-foot wide track around the perimeter of our unusually large classroom provided a safe ring for teaching rhythm through music and whole body movement. My teammate usually played the piano while I led all 60 children around the track. One morning we were enthusiastically galloping to the William Tell Overture when I tripped over a child in front of me and fell face down on the slippery waxed floor. While the children gasped in horror, the momentum of our fast gallop propelled me into the center of the room. When I sat up, unharmed except for my dignity, the children first cheered, then, in relief, broke out in uproarious laughter. They were still giggling about it when they lined up to go home at their red, yellow and blue doors and no doubt shared the event as soon as a parent asked, *What did you do at school today?*

Should we skip the draw-write-read program with so many students at one time? Instead we capitalized on the big room which had a full-sized movie screen on one wall. We arranged three groups of long tables with their short ends parallel to the screen. That way the children would only have to turn their heads to the side to see the screen. To avoid the melee of 60 children scrambling for seats with their special friends, the three tables were color-coded with their neighborhood colors, red, yellow and blue. Students found their places by large name cards. At each place we put a large sheet of newsprint and a fat black crayon.

We set up an overhead projector. One teacher drew lines on the projector bed to show the sequence of strokes for students to imitate. Holding their crayons, the students were first shown how to write a stroke in the air in the vertical orientation of the screen, then write the stroke in the air over their paper in a horizontal orientation, and finally produce the mark on their paper.

When each letter was complete we then used it as a scaffold and added a few strokes to turn it into a letter-animal representing a speech sound in English. Finally the students were given color crayons to complete their drawings. Perhaps the students had been trained by television watching at home. They seemed to be mesmerized by our overhead projector and screen. They learned faster than our former students in classes of only 30 students did.

Duane writes, *One winter day my family and me went skeing down a step hil.*

Our former kindergarten room had glass walls overlooking the playground. We could not use it because it would distract the sixth graders who now occupied our room. Instead, the only available space for outdoor play was a large grassy area with no installed equipment. Supervising 60 young children in free play would not be safe, so all outdoor play was necessarily directed. Relays seemed the best solution. So we divided each 60 into six different teams of ten and hopped, skipped, walked backward, crawled ran and all ways of locomotion we could think of. In addition to honing these physical skills, the children developed a surprising level of team spirit and camaraderie.

No evidence developed to indicate that being assigned to such large groups harmed these young students. In contrast to former school years, we recommended none of them for a second year of kindergarten. The following year the first grade teachers reported that these students were far easier to teach compared to students of former years. Their attention span seemed longer. Perhaps the large groups developed more independence.

In the interests of safety for the large numbers of students in our unique team-teaching program, it was necessary that many of our activities be directed and closely supervised. On reflection, our kindergarten was similar to Japanese kindergartens with their large teacher-pupil ratio and regimentation. Also, like the Japanese homogenous population, our students were primarily middle class Anglo children in a suburban community with high expectations for education. Not knowing what to expect of kindergarten, the children adapted.

We teachers were presented with a difficult situation, including a group of hostile parents. With intensive planning we made it work. The children survived, but we teachers did not fare so well. The following summer I had major kidney surgery. My teammate developed a severe case of psoriasis from the tension of teaching 60 children twice a day for a school year. Our great experiment was not a success for teachers. The two new schools were completed in the summer and our school went back to two classes for each kindergarten teacher, 30 students in the morning and another 30 in the afternoon.

READING SPECIALIST

After being assigned as a reading specialist in my school district I discovered that the state law did not permit me to work in my own field of interest, the prevention of reading disability, but only in remediation. Working with a state senator from my district, we wrote a bill to make it permissible for reading specialists to assist kindergarten teachers in building foundation skills for writing and reading.

I was invited to address the Senate Education Committee regarding the reading bill. Instead of listening to me, the senators laughed and talked among themselves. Remembering one of the first tenets of good teaching YOU MUST FIRST GET THEIR ATTENTION, I reached into my purse for a collection of reward badges I had saved for the children. Each one was labeled, HAPPINESS IS READING. Walking to the senators, I pinned a badge on each one, then returned to the podium and the microphone. They listened. Our bill passed.

With that heady success, I worked with our senator on two more bills affecting kindergarten. First we wrote legislation requiring schools to make room for all age-eligible children. Prior to that bill schools were allowed to accept only those children who were signed up until each class had 30 children. Next we wrote the bill eliminating the double session for each teacher, one in the morning and one in the afternoon. Finally, our bill passed setting the maximum class load of 33 children per teacher.

As a reading specialist, I met many students like Johnny and Mitchell back at Wooden Valley. By the time they met me they were convinced that they either wouldn't or couldn't learn to read. Drawing on my Wooden Valley experience, I did not attempt to teach reading to these students who had been labeled, REMEDIAL. Instead, I asked them first to draw cartoons and pictures about events in their own lives to build visual imagery and memory. Promotion of the use of the comic format with *talking balloons* over their drawings encouraged students to listen to their own speech sounds to record letters in the balloons. We studied cartoonists' special tricks for showing movement and different facial expressions. As they gained confidence, gradually students began to label their pictures, first with a single word and then longer captions. These labels grew into sentences with invented spellings by ear. As I discovered back at Wooden Valley, this independent writing gradually led to more self confidence and eventually to more successful reading, as well as more awareness of correct spelling.

Professional diagnosis of every remedial student referred to me indicated that all of them had an incomplete knowledge of our alphabetic code for the English language. They had missed the boat in kindergarten and first grade. All of them could recite the alphabet from memory. They could write the letters in alphabetical order, both in capitals and in lower case forms. They were not absolutely sure, however, which letters to use to represent the forty or more speech sounds they used in ordinary conversation. They could use picture clues in their reading without this sound-symbol knowledge, but they could not decode unknown words. Daily writing practice revealed the gaps and helped fill them in. Improved reading followed. More and more it was evident that Montessori was right when she wrote, *Show young children how to write and they will then explode spontaneously into reading.*

HEAD START

With my new Elementary Administration credential, I was selected to be the director of our first countywide HEAD START program. The question was posed to me concerning the possible segregation of the English-speaking and the Spanish-speaking children. My early Wooden Valley experience taught me that young children can quickly learn not only different languages, but also, in the process, learn to respect different cultures. The Spanish-speaking parents whom I hired as aides agreed to mix the children and they soon became minimally bilingual. That year was the beginning of a long successful career for one of those parents I hired. Eventually Esperanza (which translates to Hope) became a national leader in the Economic Opportunity program.

In addition to the children whose home language was Spanish, we enrolled two other distinct types of English-speaking children in our Head Start program. One group primarily came from single parent families and lived in low-income neighborhoods in town. These children, in general, had fluent speech, even loquacious, though some adults might classify some of their four letter words as unacceptable. The other group of English-speaking children had few neighborhood play experiences because they came from isolated ranch families. Children in this group, in general, had difficulties in understanding spoken directions, spoke themselves in very simple sentences, and frequently substituted one speech sound for another. At the end of our first summer Head Start we administered a simple preschool achievement test. The lowest scores were made not by the Spanish-speaking youngsters, but by the rural children with undeveloped English for their age.

Building on my own learning back at Wooden Valley of the importance of drawing for eye-hand coordination, visual perception and visual memory, part of each Head Start day was spent in free drawing for all the children. Like the migrants back at Wooden Valley, we discovered that the Spanish-speaking children were more advanced in drawing than either of our groups of English-speaking children. Could this be related to American parents and schools traditionally viewing art activities as frills rather than as mental training for literacy?

We took all our Head Start children on a field trip to the California coast, assuming that they would be in awe of the vast expanse of our Pacific Ocean. Instead, as soon as they reached the smooth band of wet sand they ignored the water, fell to their knees and began drawing in the sand with their fingers, sticks and shell fragments. One child delightedly found a long stick for his drawing tool, then ran around the perimeter of his project, dragging his stick to create a ten-foot long fish, complete with fins. Then, using broken shells, he added scales. Finally he searched the sand until he found a large, smooth round stone which he plopped into place for his fish's eye.

Pilots at our local airport gave all the
Head Start children a short plane ride.

One of our Head Start children rarely walked upright. Anna had very efficient locomotion by walking on all fours like an animal. It was a rapid movement, alternating right hand and left foot with the opposite pair, as in a crawl. Anna, however, was on her hands and feet, not on her hands and knees. This child's language development and play skills indicated that she was of superior intelligence. At lunchtime the animal behavior was again in evidence when Anna put her face into her plate instead of using the eating tools provided.

A home visit was clearly indicated. Early one evening I found Anna's residence, a four-story hundred-year-old Victorian home in a run-down neighborhood. On the top floor, at the end of a long dark hall through an open door, I caught sight of Anna. A younger girl and a crawling infant were playing on the bare floor with two miniature poodles, one black and one white. A young woman, probably their mother, was sleeping so soundly on a rumpled bed that I could not awaken her.

My first concern was for the baby. I felt his bare back and legs. With no clothes on except a wet diaper, his body was very cold from the hallway breeze. Should I leave this appalling scene? What was my professional responsibility? I asked Anna for a dry diaper and shirt for the baby and changed him. The room was getting darker and I saw no switch to turn on the bare bulb. There were no chairs, so I found a small blanket in a drawer to wrap the baby in and sat down on the floor with him in my lap. He stared at me with interest, but seemed to show no fear of a stranger. The little girls and the poodles took turns eating dry dog food from a bowl on the floor. They ignored me as the room got darker and darker. I didn't know what I was waiting for, except my conscience would not let me leave these three small children with no supervision.

Finally there were footsteps in the hallway. A light turned on revealing a tall, young man in clean, fashionable clothes. A handsome blond prince had come to my rescue and the children's. Introducing myself as the director of Anna's Head Start program, I told him about our curiosity and concern for her animal-like behavior. He laughed. *That's because her mother pays more attention to the poodles than to the children. The girls think that if they act like the dogs, then she might give them some attention too.*

Our discussion aroused the mother. She sat up in bed and called the dogs to her. I introduced myself, but it was soon obvious that she was either too sleepy or too drugged to understand why I was there. With the young man present, the children had a responsible adult to care for them. I found my way down the dark stairway and outside to fresh air.

Eventually Head Start was able to intervene on the children's behalf and they were placed with their grandmother. Several months later in our local newspaper I recognized the face of the handsome, responsible young man with whom I had left the children that evening. According to the newspaper account, he was accused of abducting a young woman, murdering her and leaving her body beside the road in front of my rural Wooden Valley School. How wrong I was in my judgment of his character.

CONSULTANT

A one-year assignment, half time as a primary curriculum consultant and half time doing public relations for our county schools, did nothing for my self-esteem. Because of my interest in children from rural areas, and more probably because I might initiate less controversy there, my assignment was to five outlying small schools. Principals at these schools seemed to be so protective of their turf that they discouraged any assistance to their teachers by me. One principal whose school enrolled a number of children whose home language was Spanish was particularly suspicious of me. During Head Start I had sent home communications to those families in both Spanish and English. This principal indicated that my action had undermined her long campaign that these adults should learn English.

I was delighted, however, to have the opportunity to work with the teacher at Wooden Valley, as well as with another one-room school. Johnny, who at first proclaimed, *I'M NOT GOING TO LEARN TO READ AND YOU CAN'T MAKE ME DO IT,* was now a leader both academically and socially. He was looking forward to junior high to he could be on the track team like his father.

My half time assignment in public relations was particularly difficult. My job was to report news about county schools to the local newspaper. For some reason I was deliberately excluded from attending any staff meetings. When I explained to the superintendent that to write news I needed to know what was going on. He snapped, *I DON'T CARE WHAT*

YOU WRITE—JUST PUT MY NAME IN THE FIRST SENTENCE.
Apparently I was specifically hired not for any writing skills, but primarily to build his political image.

Continuing to simmer over the first superintendent's put-down years before, *THAT IS ONLY YOUR LAY OPINION,* I passed a state civil service examination and acquired the impressive title of State Consultant in Early Childhood Education. When I was accepted in the state fold with that title I assumed that the selection process was influenced by the newly acquired initials, M.A. after my name and my reasonably high scores on the test. Instead, with my first assignment in this role I realized that my early experiences as what the journalists call a *pencil pusher* probably looked promising on my record.

The first unrealistic task given to me was to write a guide for the state's Children's Centers, outlining expectations for the other consultants, some of whom had served the department for several years. I composed my regulations four days a week. On Friday we held a meeting where I read them to the seasoned, experienced consultants. Of course they quickly exposed my naiveté, so the following week I revised and rewrote the guidelines. Eventually the official document was in print and distributed throughout the state. Why the experienced consultants didn't write their own guidelines in the first place, I never knew. In my first role as a state bureaucrat I began to feel more and more like Alice in Wonderland.

My next assignment for the State was to assist in the monitoring of Head Start projects and Children's Centers. In order to assure honest monitoring, consultants living in Northern California were assigned to monitor programs in Southern California, and vice versa. Consequently, I drove to the Sacramento airport every Monday morning and flew to Los Angeles where I was assigned to a state-owned car, often an aged station wagon. After I figured out the special intricacies of the particular vehicle and studied the map of the busy Los Angeles freeways I set out on the week's treasure hunt to find the centers assigned to me. Often it took most of the morning to find the first center on the list.

In this monitoring capacity my major tasks were to step off the square footage in each building and outdoor area, estimate the square feet of glass in the window areas, then fill out the information on the official pink forms. The number of toilets and washing areas compared to the number of children enrolled went on the green forms. The placement and date of the last inspection of the fire extinguisher went on the blue forms. After eating the official government Type A lunch, I filled out the yellow forms. Checking the list for the number of Spanish surnames, regardless of the children's spoken language, I filled out the white forms.

At the end of each day, after monitoring two or three preschools, I found a motel for the night and filled out more forms. There was no opportunity in my role for any input concerning what the children or the staff were actually doing. There was no opportunity to exercise my title role as a consultant in early childhood education, rather than as a building inspector. In spite of the fact that my salary was almost double for teaching, my consultant role was rapidly losing is appeal.

Then, in the summer months, the job briefly became more interesting. I was sent to monitor the migrant centers in California's hot central valley. While parents worked long hours in the fields picking cotton or fruit, their young children were cared for in these impressive, well-run centers. My major assignment was to encourage the caretakers to keep verbally interacting with all the children, even the infants, so they would develop language, usually Spanish. After my Wooden Valley experience where instruction from the school board told me not to waste time on the migrants, it was most rewarding to be part of a program which might make a difference in the lives of some of these young summer children.

One afternoon I was delighted to discover Marta, the oldest of our migrant students back at Wooden Valley. Marta was now a young adult and a mother to one of the infants at this center. She had learned English, in spite of her nomadic schooling. She told me that her young husband worked in the fields, but she was on the staff at this center.

I talked to Marta about my official assignment, to encourage the children to talk. I also tried to explain to her the need to try to spark their intellectual curiosity. Marta did not understand this need, so the following day I brought a small aquarium full of guppies. To model a lesson, I gathered a few children around my gift and tried to get them to answer a few questions. *Porqué las pescas son en el agua?* (Why are the fish in the water?) Everytime I used the Spanish word for *why* the children's automatic answer was a loud, *porqué NO !* Seeing my frustration, Marta explained to me that in the Mexican culture it is considered rude for children to question adults. The common parent's answer to a child's *porqué* would probably be *porqué no.* This incident reminded me of the importance of respecting and understanding other cultures in our bilingual classes. The issue is not always simply learning a second language.

One afternoon I was assigned to attend a lecture on Mexican culture. Driving to the meeting I encountered a group of dark-haired. dark-eyed boys playing ball in the street in an obviously Mexican neighborhood. The boys stood aside waiting for me to drive slowly past them. One youngster, about seven, raised his hand in a meaningful gesture by forming a circle with his thumb and forefinger. Assuming that he was indicating, A-OK, I smiled and returned the gesture. Later, at the culture meeting, the lecturer mentioned the difference between body languages in world cultures. He said the thumb and forefinger circle sign in the Mexican culture translates to an insult, *YOU ARE AN ASS HOLE.* Again I was reminded that language is not the only bridge to cross in our growing multicultural society.

My year as a state consultant was completed and I looked forward to returning to the world of teaching. Then I agreed to assist for the month of August to evaluate proposals sent in to our office by all the state-funded preschool centers. The first proposal assigned to me for evaluation was submitted by a large center in a metropolitan area. I spent a full morning reading it carefully and making notes on the strengths and weaknesses of the proposal. When I turned in my report to the assistant bureau chief he told me my work was not the task expected. *Just check the figures in the budget section with your adding machine. Staple the calculation strip to the budget page and initial it. We send these on to the State Board of Education to prove that our department has checked each proposal.*

That seemed simple enough. I could punch numbers on an adding machine, and this task didn't require any complicated math. In the back of my mind, however, I wondered why I should be expected to check the calculations of a highly qualified auditor who had probably entered the initial figures. Also I wondered why this easy task was not assigned to some clerks in the fiscal department in the adjoining office, rather than to highly paid consultants. To quote Alice, *This job was becoming curiouser and curiouser.*

To my surprise, the assignment was not that simple. My sums did not turn out to be identical with the project figures on the budget page of the proposal. I repeated the calculation over and over again, but each time there was a slight difference in my figures from those in the proposal. I hesitated to reveal my math insecurity, but finally went again to the assistant bureau chief in charge of the operation. He let me in on the secret.

We have six different brands of adding machines in our office. These are the same as the ones in the state's preschool centers. Each machine they use may have a slightly different level of mathematical sophistication. What you need to do is find a machine in our office which will give you the exact figure to the decimal as the one used by the original auditor involved with the proposal you are working on. Now this game was a treasure hunt! Then I knew I really was in Wonderland and the assistant bureau chief was the Mad Hatter.

Faithfully following his directions for the month, I then left my brief role as a bureaucrat with no regrets and gladly returned to my school district in Napa Valley. In my haste to return to the real world on my last day in the capital, I was flagged down by a highway patrol officer for speeding. When I heard the siren and saw the flashing lights behind me I pulled over to the side of the road while all the frustrations of the year exploded. When the officer approached I blurted out through my tears, *You can't know how frustrating it is to work for the State. I'm just trying to get out of here!* He laughed, *Yes, I do. I'm a state employee too.* And he tore up my ticket with the warning, *Now slow down so you'll get home in one piece.*

NON-GRADED PRIMARY SCHOOL

Back in Napa Valley, I was delighted to be assigned to another rural school, though this one was not one room, but two. It was in an isolated pocket canyon formed long ago by an earthquake fault with no exit at the far end of the canyon. Families who lived farthest away, about ten miles from the school, infrequently came over the narrow mountain road to town.

It was evident that a number of these canyon children exhibited the same undeveloped immature language as the rural Head Start children. Two more groups of children were also similar to other Head Start groups, some with adequate language development from a nearby suburban housing area, and a few whose home language was Spanish.

My major assigned responsibility was for teaching all subjects to students in the first and second grades. My co-worker was the teacher for the third and fourth grades. Fresh from college, Sandra was open to innovation and exceptionally knowledgeable about how to teach the New Math, my weak area.

Sandra agreed to come into my room to teach math to my younger students while I took her older group for writing, reading and spelling activities. Next we tried team-teaching the same subject to all grades at the same time. That way Sandra did all the math planning and major instruction to all four grades while I followed her directions, functioning as her teacher aide. I gradually began to feel more comfortable teaching math. The other half of the morning we switched roles. I was then the major teacher for writing, reading and spelling and she was my aide. That way all students had the benefit of the strengths of each teacher.

Another benefit, which I had learned back at Wooden Valley, was that the youngest Spanish-speaking children from their family-oriented culture were not segregated by age. Their older siblings were always in sight. Most of all, we teachers gained valuable information from each other.

With our innovative approaches we both discovered that some of the older students, particularly those from isolated ranches, needed the more basic instruction being taught to the younger children. In addition, a few of the younger children were ready for more advanced instruction than their grade level assignment. We were teaching the same content twice, and inefficiently. We then regrouped the students by achievement levels, ignoring both their assigned grade levels and their birth dates. No group had an age spread of more than three years; the same spread in which children naturally group themselves for neighborhood play. By adapting to these children's needs we gradually evolved through trial and error into a departmentalized ungraded primary school.

Some of the parents who lived at the far end of the canyon reported that there was an eight-year-old boy living up there who had never been to school. The county attendance officer, an ex-Marine, went up to check on the boy, but left in a hurry, dodging bullets from the boy's father's shotgun. The county school nurse then put on her white coat and bravely approached the ranch. She convinced the family that the boy should come to school.

The following week when his 18-year-old sister brought the boy to school she mentioned that she had not been to school since the second grade. Through a county work-study program we were able to hire Katrina as our aide. She proved to be a valuable playground director, nature study expert and art teacher. While acting as our aide, Katrina learned along with our primary students the basic academic skills that she had missed. Several times in conversation Katrina mentioned that her family was of royal blood, but we teachers assumed that she was fantasizing. Many years later in an obituary notice for the mother of the family we learned that she had been a Dutch princess who had been banned because she married a commoner.

To relieve any parents' anxiety about our alternative program we invited them to an evening meeting, which turned into a standing-room-only crowd. We teachers explained the reasons for our regrouping by the students' academic needs rather than by their birth certificates. In addition we told the parents that we had departmentalized by the particular strengths of the teachers. The parents agreed to our arrangement and requested that we keep the kindergarten age students the following year and bus the fourth graders to town instead.

We invited parents to visit whenever they came by the school on the way to town. And they did! We were surprised to discover how comfortable these rural parents were in a teaching role when they volunteered as our aides. Many of them had previously led groups of children in 4-H activities. They read stories to children, listened to beginners read, brought farm animals to share, cooked with the children and supervised learning games. They also helped with time-consuming filing tasks such as keeping each child's portfolio up-to-date. Soon we teachers had to schedule parents as well as teachers.

We discovered that it was easier to teach a three-year age span than the traditional American twelve months graded span. In the latter system teachers commonly divide a class into high, middle and low learning groups, a subtle tracking system which usually labels children throughout their school life. Regardless of the labels used, once a turtle always a turtle. With our three-year span we had the same three groups, but they were of mixed ages.

Students moved ahead at flexible, different rates, taking three, four or five years to complete the four-year primary curriculum expectations without being labeled either *gifted* or *slow learner.* When the top group moved on to the fourth grade at a larger school, the middle and lower groups moved up a step, leaving room for a new crop of beginners. Every child eventually had a chance to be in the top group. At this level they were given the opportunity to be peer tutors for part of each day.

One year the National Education Association voted to search the nation for outstanding education projects instead of having their annual conference. Our Soda Canyon ungraded primary project was one of the schools selected and a flood of visitors followed. Often they would comment, *This school looks like a parent cooperative preschool.* Our considerable parent involvement was a direct outgrowth of my own experience both in preschool and in Head Start.

Though I was now completely qualified with an administrative credential, the superintendent assigned a principal from a larger school each year to oversee our innovative operations. Mr.Arnold, the principal whom I had unfortunately embarrassed some years before when he objected to the team kindergarten for his daughter, must have volunteered to be the first. He came every Friday afternoon, put his feet up on my desk and announced, *This program has to go. It will never work!* Fortunately he did not stay long each time he came.

When we began our ungraded program only two of the second grade students could read at all and few of the third grade students were independent readers. It was necessary that much of our instruction in all subjects use a hands-on approach rather than the textbook approach that had not been successful with them. We made use of our local sources for science and social studies. In the Fall we did a whole school unit on apples. We took walking field trips to nearby ranches to pick different varieties of apples. Back in the classroom we compared them by size, shape, color, taste and texture. Several parents supervised the students in making applesauce and apple pies. A father helped some of our older students build apple drying trays which we put on the school roof to prevent sampling by the deer when school was not in session. We took a field trip to the local apple cider factory, then wrote and illustrated our experiences.

We took walking field trips to nearby ranches
to pick different varieties of apples.

We went to the
appl sider factory
It was woshing
appls. The appls wr
in the wotr And
after we woched
the appls we had
a drinc uv sum
applsidre.
Charlie Thomson. 7 yr. 1 mo.

Charlie wrote about the apple cider factory.

One day my teammate brought in a plastic bowling set. A parent donated a strip of hall carpet to reduce the noise. Voila! An ideal game for introducing the concept of subtraction was born. Practicing number combinations up to ten in a motivating context became a major pastime.

Parents seemingly were not concerned with our ignoring ages and grade levels for instruction. Frequently they reported to us the children's usual answer when strangers in town asked them what grade they were in. Commonly the children would answer, *I don't know. I go to primary school.*

One stormy morning during the second year of our project I arrived at school to find that lightning had knocked out our electricity. We could conduct school without lights, but our well would not operate without electricity. Sixty small children and no running water for toilets for a whole day was not feasible. I tried to reach the currently assigned principal, but the telephone was not operating. I had to make my own administrative decision. I knew, from my Wooden Valley experience, that according to the state education code we would not lose any funding for the day if the students spent some brief time in the building. As each bus arrived I told the driver to wait while the children came in the building for about ten minutes. Then they boarded the bus and went home. At midmorning when the power was restored I called the principal to report my action in the emergency. Instead of praise, I received a tirade of abuse because he thought we would lose funding. Not knowing the legal regulations for such situations, he demanded that I phone a few families who lived nearest the school and request that their children return. We had six students for the rest of the day.

The principal assigned to us for our third year visited one afternoon. Sandra was sharing some new game with him in our math area while all sixty students were on the floor in my room for story time. In the middle of my story Sandra burst in and dismissed all the children to the playground. I knew by her face that we had an emergency. *Harry has passed out in the math room!* Sure enough, our principal was obviously unconscious and breathing heavily with his six-foot body stretched across some of the students' low tables. I dialed 911 immediately and in ten minutes an ambulance took Harry away while the excited students watched through the fence. Meanwhile I reported our actions to the superintendent who then chided me for not first asking permission before I called for help. We teachers were never told what Harry's problem was. He was soon replaced with another principal.

At the beginning of the next school year the school district gave some parents the option of bringing their primary level children to our mixed age program if it had been recommended that they be retained in a grade level in their own attendance area. Six families accepted the option. With our grouping by achievement, rather than by age or grade level, we were able to mainstream these children into our program so they did not stand out from the others, except for Terry. He was already seven years old and large for his age. In two years of kindergarten he had acquired no basic skills in foundations for academics, or in necessary socialization. We grouped Terry with our new beginners and amazingly he began to pay attention to some of our instruction. His street language was full of four letter epithets, but the other students seemed to understand that he just didn't know that such words were unacceptable at school. His language was not contagious and no parents objected to Terry's presence. The children took turns helping him learn some basics and eventually he could read about first grade level. After a year with us his parents decided he needed to be with older children. So they took him to a larger school where he was placed in a special education class.

One day we were playing a pass-it-on whispering game. I noticed the pained expressions on the faces of our rural children whose articulation was so poor. One child, unsure of the task, was turning blue from holding his breath. I realized then that these children could not whisper. Most of their communication was with vowel sounds. Analyzing the dilemma, I realized that when we whisper our consonant sounds are emphasized and vowels are suppressed. We did not have an assigned speech therapist for our school, so we devised a daily lip-reading game with exaggerated mouth positions. Every child played the game. Articulation dramatically improved.

My role as the major language arts teacher for our primary school was to find a successful way to teach writing and reading to these rural children whose oral language was below age expectation. I tried the animal noise, draw-write-read program that had worked so well back at Wooden Valley. Again the program was contagious. Even Terry began to write letters and then add drawing strokes to turn the letters into animals making familiar speech noises. A group of mothers made a set of 26 beanbags in the shapes of the letter-animals. Beginners learned to blend the animal sounds together into words through beanbag tossing games.

Mothers made a set of letter-animal beanbags
for blending into words.

Gradually these young children began to reduce their letter-animal drawings into only the letters and joined them into words.

Emily writes, *mom and I rode or bics.*

Andrea writes, *I was sing ing out sid.*

Jenny writes, *We lisend to a store uboWt robins.*

David writes, *A fiyr truc went to the mowntins
to put the fiyr out.*

Eileen writes, *Jessica and I plad duc duc gos.*

Dayna writes, *My frends and I plad on the jungljim.*

Yvonne writes, *I am hanin up sid don on the swin set.*

Kirsten writes, *I wus sic in bed. I Plad wiv my dols.*

These early writers could remember and tell you what they had written. But when I checked several days later I discovered that they had not retained those memories and could not read back their stories. As Montessori had written in the early years of the last century, I also discovered that decoding was obviously more difficult that encoding. However, we continued to encourage their daily drawing and writing. Their stories became longer and more elaborated. As they gained more confidence and more practice some of the students switched from simple autobiographical experiences to imaginary stories—from simple reporting to fiction.

Chris writes this cliff-hanger story. *The lion was singking in quicksand. The lion omost got out of the quicksand. Then the lion started to singking more in the quicksand. Fily no mor lion.*

We discovered that these children could write book reports long before they could read the books.

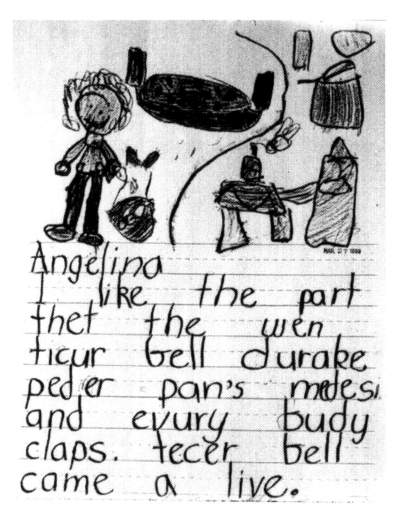

Angelina

I like the part
thet the wen
ticur bell durake
peder pan's medes.
and evury budy
claps. tecer bell
came a live.

Their writing was always a noisy process, saying words aloud sound by sound and writing letters representing what they heard. Magically these independent writers then began to spontaneously read with minimal instruction. What happened? I read that the right side of the brain's cortex controls designs such as letters. The left side controls speech sounds and language comprehension. I wondered, could it be that this early writing practice had stimulated the two sides of the brain to work together in concert and produce reading?

Jeremy was our exception. The youngest child from a large family in which the father was a school psychologist, Jeremy was certainly not a conformist. He refused to participate in any beginning writing activities. When it was outside playtime, Jeremy stayed in. When it was time to come inside, Jeremy went out. One morning I was reading a story to my group and noticed Jeremy crawling under some desks until he reached some low bookshelves. There he picked up a do-it-yourself workbook for a programmed reader set, found a pencil and filled in the blanks for the next two hours. At dismissal time Jeremy asked to take a book home. So I selected an easy preprimer with the Dick and Jane format which repeats words and phrases. The next morning Jeremy came in and slammed the book down on my desk with, *This book says the same thing over and over. I GET IT THE FIRST TIME.* After that I let Jeremy choose his own books and shortly he could read any book in our library.

An intern teacher from the University was assigned to us for training. Her supervisor, who frequently visited our school, later was secretary to the task force that developed the state's exemplary early childhood program. They used our school as the model. It took no extra funding to run our mixed age primary school. We simply grouped students in more fair, more considerate and more efficient ways than the common practice of grouping students by their birth certificates. Also, instead of first designing a curriculum and then trying to fit children into it, we developed a curriculum around the specific needs of individual enrolled children.

The word of our success spread and parents from other school attendance areas tried to enroll their children with us. According to our space we were limited to 60 children. So parents camped out all night on the school grounds to be among the first in line on enrollment day.

Administrators still did not understand or approve of our program. They could not calculate attendance in traditional ways because we did not attach grade levels to our students. In addition, administrators were unable to figure out a way to order materials for us unless we grouped students by their birth certificates. It seemed that it was more important to them to count children rather than to teach them.

The other elementary principals who still used the archaic age-graded system also did not appreciate our success. Parents in their attendance areas requested transfer of their children to our successful program. Six years after we began our innovation the school district's population dropped. The principals to whom we were a threat then convinced the school board that larger schools were more economical. They did not consider the cost to society of our age-graded schools. They can cause so many children to become such misfits that they drop out and become the unemployed, the underemployed, or those with major social problems. Political pressure from the other elementary principals then convinced the school board to close our model school.

RESEARCH STUDY

Stunned by the closure of our successful school which had been recognized by the National Education Association and replicated by the State's Early Childhood Education program, I decided I needed more credibility. Perhaps I needed more of those special letters after my name. I accepted another assignment as a reading specialist. This would be less time-consuming and I could complete my doctoral degree which I had begun working on several years before.

For my final thesis the school board gave me permission to conduct a comparative study of all the kindergarten students in the district. The major objective of this long term field study was to determine whether or not teaching kindergarten students to WRITE independent compositions would make a significant difference in their readiness to READ.

Traditional expectations of American kindergarten students include a variety of pre-reading tasks, depending upon the teacher's philosophy, administrative decree, or the published program used. These are presumed to be foundation skills for the reading program which follows. The variety includes:

- Naming alphabet letters, either upper or lower case, or both,
- Copying alphabet letters, either upper or lower case, or both,

- Memorizing alphabet order, through visual or auditory channels or both,
- Recognizing speech sounds that are alike, either in isolation, or in beginning, medial or ending positions in spoken words,
- Rhyming ending syllables by ear,
- Matching alphabet letters to speech sounds and the reverse,
- Recognizing by sight of common printed words, such as students names, color names, numeral names and common nouns and verbs.

My study proposed that if all of the above pre-reading activities were replaced instead with directed WRITING activities, such as:

- Encouraging every pupil to draw every day, in order to record real or imagined experiences (to build symbolic activity, visual imagery and the necessary eye-hand coordination for writing),
- Writing single alphabet letters from dictation of their most common speech sounds,
- Writing syllables and short words with common regular spelling patterns from dictation,
- Writing independent compositions with invented spellings (self dictation with emphasis on writing the speech sounds said aloud, rather than dependence on visual or auditory memory of letter sequence in words),

Would students reverse the process of ENCODING to DECODING? Would they figure out how to read without direct instruction in reading, or pressure from home or school to do so?

Nineteen teachers volunteered to participate in the write-to-read study which I had begun to investigate back at Wooden Valley in return for a set of materials Their classes were taught with my draw-write-read program turning letters into noisy animals.

The emphasis was on showing beginners how to form lower case letters and the speech sounds represented by the letters so they could independently record anything they could say. The University granted ten units to these teachers who would assist in the development of the program by using it in their classes for one school year.

Twenty-six teachers comprised the control group. Their classes were taught with a variety of traditional published readiness materials of their own choice. All students in both groups were pretested at the beginning of their school years with a standard kindergarten achievement test and post-tested for their growth at the end. The result was significantly in favor of the alternative approach.

One surprising outcome of my year-long study showed that the students who scored lowest at the beginning of their kindergarten year made the most growth in beginning literacy with a draw-write-read approach. They scored 190 percent higher in word reading and 213 percent higher in sentence reading than the control group. Apparently this is a suitable approach for kindergarten children who are at risk for failure. The following examples from the study show the remarkable progress of these five-year-olds who were independently writing and spelling by ear before any traditional reading or spelling instruction.

Wendy
I am niding mi frend s
hors in the gras.

Kirsten P.
I had spugete for lunch.

Jimmy
I am geting wet
and have ing fun.

Matt
I am throing a bol for
Ru thr frd.

Jesse
I am Play with mi dog.

Cameron
DUtch and I Practist socr
and tenis.

The write-to-read students in the study kept their lead. Five years later the children who had first been taught with the draw-write-read approach in kindergarten scored higher than the district norm on their fifth grade achievement test in both spelling and reading. This indicated positive long-term effects for stressing drawing and writing before young children are expected to read.

Will these students spell phonetically by ear forever? Yes, they will. So will students taught originally with more traditional memory approaches unless, beginning in first grade, they are taught the basic rules and generalizations of English spelling. Then all students regardless of their original instruction can correctly spell innumerable words from a single pattern instead of having to memorize each word.

Emily, in the following example, has already learned to use two spelling rules: to use *ck* at the end of short vowels (*sick*), and to use the letter, *e*, at the end of words to indicate a long vowel sound (*home*). She has already memorized the spelling of the word, *was*, which does not follow a standard

English pattern. As for her phonetic spelling of the word, *diarrhea*, her teacher has unrealistically and unfairly circled it. Emily was only six years old when she created this story. When she can read about third grade level she will then have the research skills to look up the spelling of foreign words which we spell according to the spelling rules of the language from which we have borrowed them.

CONCLUSION

I never met either of my original early career goals as a trapeze performer or as a war correspondent. I did, however, go to dangerous places and write about my adventures. My dangerous places were not far away, but in my own community, in the schools. I was very wrong when I thought a career in the Education field would be dull. On reflection, my twenty-five years in the trenches as a teacher were more exciting than flying through the air with the greatest of ease or dodging bullets in a war.

My short-term memory becomes ever shorter with time. To meet appointments I must check my calendar several times a day. On the other hand, my long-term memories become ever more vivid. My first teaching experience in those special education classes was over forty years ago. Yet, in my mind's eye, I can still see Tom, the deaf child, Jenny, the blind child, and Jimmy who jumped in the creek. I can see that first class where they locked me in the closet with the spiders and then flooded the room. I can see Robert with his burn scars and those 120 students in our team-taught kindergarten.

I can see the senator who worked with me to write legislation and then arranged for me to testify before the Senate Education Committee whose members ignored me until I gave them badges to wear.

I can see that Alice in Wonderland place where I was writing the guidelines for the state's Children's Centers and measuring floor space with my consultant title. I can see those outstanding summer migrant infant centers and preschools where I found a grown-up Marta.

I can see Anna who walked on all fours like an animal in our county's first Head Start program and the murderer whom I wrongly classified as a responsible parent. I can see our successful mixed age primary school where we mainstreamed the special education students, which was recognized nationally as outstanding and was the model for the state's Early Childhood Education program.

My year at Wooden Valley taught me more than all the Education courses and advanced degrees put together. Johnny and Mitchell taught me to encourage independent writing before expecting reading. They taught me that spelling by ear is a foundation for spelling conventionally.

Wooden Valley taught me to use parent aides for invaluable public relations. It taught me to promote bilingual education through grouping together young students whose home languages and cultures are different from each other.

Wooden Valley is where I learned to use peer tutoring because teaching another is one of the best ways to learn. I learned to use social studies and science from the environment rather than from a textbook. I learned to use curriculum from each student's diagnosed needs in positive recognition of natural human variance rather than from a prepared list of graded activities.

I learned that when what is taught matches each student's needs, using developmentally appropriate activities, then discipline problems will be nonexistent. There were no discipline problems at Wooden Valley or at Soda Canyon where I practiced what I learned at Wooden Valley. Most of all, the Wooden Valley school board's wise assignment, that I help the children like going to school, also worked for me. I have fond memories of Wooden Valley.

In succeeding years I used what I learned at Wooden Valley about mixed age grouping. This fosters democracy and develops cooperation, caring and respect rather than the competition evident in our graded school systems where we divide children by their birth certificates instead of by their needs.

The following pairs of students have birthdays within several months of each other and were assigned to the same graded classroom.

Should we expect the same gross-motor tasks of each pair? Obviously, with their wide physical differences, this would not be fair. This natural spread of sizes is assumed to be natural human variance. There is just as much, or more, natural human difference in what they know and what they need to know. However, because they are close in age, our outmoded, unfair and inefficient graded system would unrealistically expect the same performance of them.

At the beginning of the last century our country was receiving thousands of immigrants speaking various languages. School administrators were faced with the problem of placing the young ones in our schools. Their solution—divide them into groups called grades by their birth certificates. If some children do not progress satisfactorily it is assumed that the children have failed rather than the system has failed to meet their needs. During the last century we have acquired a wealth of studies about child development. Yet, we still act as if all we know about young children is their birth certificates.

In our mixed age program at Soda Canyon the students varied from rural children living at the end of a ten-mile pocket canyon with few social contacts to children from the prestigious Silverado Country Club area with numerous social advantages. These social differences widened even more their natural human diversity. My team mate and I ignored their birthdays and grouped children instead by what they knew and needed to know. They moved through the four-year early primary curriculum at their own pace without the trauma of either retention or grade skipping because there were no grades. No children moved to the fourth grade at the bigger school until we knew they could function satisfactorily at that level.

Our program grouping was similar to the American Red Cross swimming program which seems to work for everybody. That organization keeps classes within a three-year span of ages. But each class is segregated by what skills children can perform, not what months they have been alive.

Our highest courts have decreed that it is illegal and unfair to segregate students by race or ethnic difference. It is just as unfair for us to continue graded school systems that segregate young students into twelve-month blocks by their birth certificates. Then, ignoring their natural human differences, we unrealistically and unfairly expect the same performance of all.

Some states today are considering legislation to consider the consequences of grade retention or social promotion. Some individuals are in favor of limiting advancing students to the next grade until they have mastered certain expected skills. Yet the Education establishment will quote research indicating that such practice fails to raise achievement. As we demonstrated at Soda Canyon, there is an alternative.

Recently in the news a report stated that *Statistics show that the typical American is not a proficient writer.* Anyone who couldn't have predicted the results of this study must have spent the last three or four decades in a cave. What happened? No, the problem is not television or the invasion of computers. In the olden days schools were expected to teach the 3 R's— *Reading, Riting and Rithmetic.* Today achievement tests at all levels cover only Reading and Math. Writing is not tested. Teachers will not spend time on what is not tested.

The demise of the second R began in 1956 with the launching of the International Reading Association. The founders, and most of the subsequent officers of this organization were and are the authors of school reading programs. They have been amazingly successful in convincing American parents of the importance of reading to their own children daily. That profitably sells books.

There is no International Writing Association to tell parents and teachers that they should also frequently draw and write with their young children to develop foundation skills for reading. There is little profit in selling paper and pencils, so writing and especially expecting young children to write before they read in their first year of school is not promoted.

Currently our nation spends millions of dollars on remediation of illiteracy. Certainly we need to continue to do so. But it is time to pay attention to prevention as well. It is time to make a change in the roots of illiteracy, the beginnings. For models today's school reformers need to look back at the one-room schools of long ago, like Wooden Valley.

In my twenty-fifth year of teaching I was observing in a kindergarten classroom. Two little boys noticed that I was watching them complete a puzzle. The red-haired boy asked his dark-skinned friend, *Is that your mother?* The little black boy laughed so hard that he fell off his chair. Joining in their joke, I assumed that he could see, with my fair coloring, I probably would not be his mother. Still chuckling, he then turned to his friend, *My mom's not an old lady.* It was time to retire.

Bibliography

Beery; Keith, *Revised Test of Visual Motor Integration.* Chicago: Follett Publishing, 1981.

Bissex, Glenda. *GNYS AT WRK.* Cambridge: Harvard University Press, 1980.

Bredecamp, Sue. *Developmentally Appropriate Practice in Early Childhood Programs.* Washington, D.C.: N.A.E.Y.C., 1987.

Chomsky, Carol. "Writing Before Reading Eighty Years Later." In Loeffler, *Montessori in Contemporary American Culture.* Portsmouth, N.J.: Heinemann, 1992.

Clay, Marie. *Writing Begins at Home.* Aukland, New Zealand. Heinemann, 1987.

Connell, Donna Reid. *Writing is Child's Play.* Addison-Wesley, 1995, Napa, CA.: Can Do Books, 2001.

—————————*Integrated Total Language (itl).* Addison-Wesley,1995. Napa, CA.: Can Do Books, 1999.

Gentry, J.Richard. "Developmental Aspects of Learning to Spell." Novato, CA.: *Academic Therapy:* Vol.20, No.1, 1984.

Graves, Donald and Virginia Stuart. *Write From the Start.* New American Library, 1985.

Henderson, Edmund. *Teaching Spelling.* Boston: Houghton Mifflin, 1985.

Olson, David. *Cognitive Development, The Child's Acquisition of Diagonality.* New York: Academic Press, 1970.

Platt, Penny. "Grapho-linguistics: Children's drawings in relation to reading and writing skills." *The Reading Teacher,* December, 1977.

Read, Charles. *Children's Creative Spelling.*London: Routledge & Kegan Paul, 1986.

Stanford Achievement Test Series. SESAT 1, SESAT 2. New York: Harcourt Brace Jovanovich, 1983,

• Developmentally appropriate activities
for individuals functioning at the 4 to 8
age maturity levels

• Teaches letters as pictures of noisy animals, similar to
Laubach's highly successful world-wide picture-letter
program for adults.

• Plus Writing is Childs Play, a 127 page
explicit parent-teacher guide telling
WHY, WHAT and HOW to enhance
these important literacy skills.

Send for BOTH *itl* and the guide for 75.00, plus shipping

2119 Lone Oak Avenue
Napa, CA., 94558
707-224-0197

In this memoir Dr. Connell remembers teaching belligerent Johnny who declared, I'M NOT GOING TO LEARN TO READ AND YOU CAN'T MAKE ME DO IT, the principal who passed out in her class room and other challenging events. She discovered that the teaching business is certainly not dull. Her first career was as a journalist. Her pre-marital byline, Donna Reid, in a West Coast magazine was lifted by an agent who was seeking a stage name for a fledgling actress. Dr. Connell's other claim to fame is inventing the hole in Cheerios during her role in the advertising field. After W.W.II she and her husband moved to a rural area to raise their four young children in a safe tranquil environment. This led to an egg business with 3000 cooperating hens. Their neighbor, a school superintendent, recruited both of them to be teachers, though neither them had experience in that field. Donna acquired that know-how as a teacher-principal of a one-room school. Later she applied the one-room attributes by pioneering multi-age grouping and using parent-aides at a larger school which became the model for the state's early childhood program. Her favorite activity is showing young children how to compose and write their own original thoughts. Then, to everyone's surprise, they explode spontaneously into reading. Today she serves as a consultant for that write-to-read approach to literacy.